LULLABIES, LEGENDS AND LIFE

– The Quest for Contentment –

First published 2014 by DB Publishing, an imprint of JMD Media Ltd, Nottingham, United Kingdom.

ISBN 9781780914589

LULLABIES, LEGENDS AND LIFE

– The Quest for Contentment –

EAMON KAVANAGH

CONTENTS

ACKNOWLEDGEMENTS

Great efforts by my friend Nicola Buckle, my sister Kathleen Clucas and my spiritual daughter Kelly Smith ensured this book was transformed from its original illegible scrawl into a presentable manuscript, for which I remain forever thankful.

A big thank you to DB Publishing for their wonderful support for an enthusiastic but naive writer.

Eternal thanks to the many characters, who simply by being themselves, have inspired my imagination.

Love to all my family, my lovely cousins over in the 'Emerald Isle' and of course the special folk of Bury to whom I owe so much.

A very special mention for my cousin Ellen Lynch, who was brave enough to tackle the handwritten manuscript for my first book *Pride and Passion in Bury*. Heartfelt thanks Ellen.

1.

2010

"Well! Eamon it's conclusive, you are diabetic."

Initially the information my doctor imparted to me worried me a little. His next words certainly gave me cause for concern.

"It's not the end of the world Eamon."

I'm thinking, "seems a bit over the top". My little knowledge of diabetes held no horror stories. Dr Chaudhury was to enlighten me.

"Diabetes Eamon is a degenerative disease. I am giving you the worst-case scenario. Badly managed diabetes affects most of your organs."

I can honestly say his next words terrified me.

"The first organs put under severe pressure are the eyes, ending in blindness. The reason being is that the tiny blood vessels connected to your eyes cannot deal with thickened blood."

My doctor knew by my face that he had frightened me.

"I have deliberately given you cause for worry Eamon. Too many people take diabetes too lightly. Make no mistake it should not be and with your heart problem we cannot afford to be lax. Now for the positive side: initially we will see if we can manage it by your diet; failing that, we will move to medication. To be honest Eamon I cannot believe this result. You are so slim."

"Well Doctor Chaudhury I probably haven't helped myself. I tend to binge on food and drink. It's not unknown for me to down three bottles of wine. Plus eating a family bar of chocolate in one sitting is not unheard of."

Doctor Chaudhury looked doubtful. With no history of this disease in my family, I was flummoxed. My first appointment with a dietician was arranged. Knowledge is power so they say. I thank Doctor Chaudhury who just happens to be a mighty fine doctor.

I headed home with a whole lot of mixed thoughts and emotions. Sat down with a cup of tea and chewed everything over with Dawn, my wife. A couple of thoughts passed through my mind that instinct told me to take note of. Firstly, although Royal Mail had been good enough to place me on probably the easiest round at their Wellington Street office in Bury – Stephen Street, I was still struggling to complete my round. Secondly, I was determined to gather as much information as possible about this disease that had the potential to seriously affect my health. In the end Dawn and I came up with a game plan. It was a plan that gave me comfort, as I would be doing all I could to safeguard myself from the worst advance effects of this disease.

A couple of weeks later I was sat in front of a Royal Mail nurse who advised me it would be in my interests to terminate my employment with Royal Mail on ill health grounds. I must say her advice was a shock to my system. Like most of the folk I know I had always worked, lucky enough to never be out of work. The thought of having no gainful employment worried me.

After long discussions with the folk that mattered it was decided that I should take the nurse's advice. Not doing so could prove problematic. The following Monday I informed my manager of my decision. It warmed my heart to listen to him pleading with me to think again. Pleading is probably a bit strong. I cannot think of a more suitable word. Hopefully you get my drift! It was decided I would finish on the last Friday in March.

That last day was quite an emotional one! Some of the folk on my round were genuinely upset about me leaving, which in turn upset me. Many gifts and promises of staying in touch were sworn. That day I had taken a set of clothes to change into at the end of my day so that I could leave my uniform behind.

Thankfully this would not be my last link with Royal Mail. Each year I organised a 'Young Uns versus Old Uns' football match and also the night out known as 'The Sad Lads Night Out'. This was born from an evening a few years before when a few of us posties were sat in our local with several of us drowning our sorrows in ale. On this occasion the four of us were upset. For whatever reason, our relationships with either our wives or partners had finished, leaving us feeling very sorry for ourselves. A passing comment from one of our unaffected colleagues was, "what a set of sad lads". There you have it. That first outing resulted in seven of us becoming 'Drunken Knights'. The following year there were around sixty of us so the Sad Lad's night out became Bury Posties Lads and Girls Christmas Do which is always held on the Saturday before Christmas.

Well I worked hard on my diet. Alas it was no use and I found myself on medication. Tough but what do you do? The main thing my doctor had told me was, "if you can, try not to retire to bed with high sugar readings". The wisdom of this advice was obvious, even to a dull boy like me: many hours for my thickened blood to do its damage! As a precaution against this I either took to my exercise bike for an hour or, with 60's music playing, donned my boxing gloves and pretended I was Rocky Balboa for an hour. I cannot tell you how happy I was that these sessions really helped. Not just for my diabetes but my mental state also improved.

2.

WHAT TO DO NEXT

I have always been happiest when I am active. Don't get me wrong, Sunday's these last couple of years have become lazy days. I enjoy the decadent feeling of being sat up in bed with the Sunday mags, a brew and a bacon butty. But I needed a project to keep my mind occupied. I do my own DIY around the house but these tended to be short-term projects. So one Monday evening I sat in our dimly lit living room staring into the flames of the gas fire between the coals looking for inspiration. Many things passed through my mind. Voluntary work appealed as I had already worked for Victim Support. My thoughts were interrupted by the phone ringing.

"Hello, what have you rung me for?" I was dropped on.

"Hang on, you rang me!"

"I don't think so".

I started to doubt myself now and became a little worried. "Are you messing me about or what? Who is this?"

There then followed a short giggling session, after which I said, "I'm hanging up now".

"Where's your sense of humour gone Eamon? It's Barry, Barry Edge." Barry and his brother David were my ex work colleagues at Royal Mail. Dyed in the wool Bury supporters, very keen cricket fans and really good lads. (I never got it with cricket).

"I will forgive you Baz, what can I do for you?"

"What you up to?"

"Oh just trying to think of something to keep me occupied for a while."

"Well Eamon, what am I always telling you?"

"What?"

"To write a book. All the stories you know. I tell you now I would buy it and I know most of 'em!"

This was true. Baz had on numerous occasions advised me to do just that. "You know Baz, you might just be right".

"By the way Eamon, have you got your Margaret's number?"

"Yeah, now why would you want that Baz?"

"Don't worry, just going to ask her if she fancies going for a drink".

What could I say, they are both adults.

After giving Baz our Margaret's number, he thanked me and said, "see you soon".

So, great idea thanks Baz. My only problem was that I had never written anything apart from a couple of poems to the girls I had known and there was plenty of room for improvement! So, with an unpromising beginning I would begin on a journey in stories built around the life of an average lad (me) growing up in a grand little town, (Bury) from the 60s up to what was then the present.

After completing the book in early 2012, I confess I had my doubts. Some of the tales I knew were interesting but – and it was a big but – had I been able to convert these grand stories into tales that were well enough written so as to not lose any of their potency. Plus there was quite a lot of footy in *Pride and Passion in Bury*. Obviously attractive to the footy lads, not so sure about the ladies. My next task would be to find a publisher reckless enough to take me on and try to sell to the public the ramblings of an uneducated, failed footballer. Here is where my brother Michael comes in. He composed a letter that built my book up to the point where even I would not have recognised it. He then sent around ten copies of this letter to various publishers. Five rejections followed. A few never bothered to reply.

Then, when we thought it was a lost cause, Bingo! DB Publishing asked me to send them a sample. After doing so, there again followed a tense, very long wait. I then received a letter from DBP asking me to send them the whole draft. The problem was they asked me to send it to them via email! At this time our house contained no computer. Very quickly a computer was purchased.

Luckily for me, Dawn was familiar with the workings of these strange machines. Help with my poor grammar, full stops, apostrophes etcetera – not my strong point, came from my lovely Irish cousin Ellen and my two lovely sisters Sheila and Kathleen. The photos were arranged by my wonderful daughter Megan. I am so grateful to them all.

At the beginning my book came out as an eBook. This in itself didn't fare well. I then had an interview on Manchester Radio with a lady I really respected, one Heather Scott, who due to her gift for relaxing guests, I really enjoyed. We had a rare old chat and a good giggle. My mate Paul Leach who had driven me to Media City in Salford Quays told me, "I really enjoyed it Eamon! You came across really well."

The Bury Times also covered the story. So I cannot complain it was not well advertised. The thing was, most of my friends told me that although they wanted to read my book they were not prepared to shell out around £100 for one of those silly Kindles in order to read it. What could I say? I myself would need to purchase one of those silly kindles just so I could read my own book. So that was that! I came to the conclusion that the chances of my book selling well were a pipe dream.

A couple of months later Nicky from DBL phoned me on my mobile. At the time I was enjoying a walk with my mate Leachy, taking in the many interesting sights found around the area known as "Birtle".

"Hello, its Nick".

"Hi Nick, how's it going cocker?"

"Good Eamon, you?"

"Grand!"

"Just thought I had better let you know, we are putting your book out in paperback."

For a moment I honestly lost the power of speech.

"Eamon, you there?"

"Sorry Nick" I replied, "I don't understand. I don't think hardly any of my mates have Kindles. You have blown me away Nick. I just cannot believe it".

"Eamon, you are forgetting your book is on the World Wide Web. Think of all of the Bury folk who have left the town to settle elsewhere, many abroad".

"I can honestly say this is the best news I have had in a long time," I replied excitedly. "Thanks so much".

It wasn't long before a book signing was arranged at Waterstones in the precinct in Bury town centre. It would take a better writer than me to convey how I felt on that wonderful day. A table was set out with two piles of my books to one side. Dawn and members of my family were in attendance. Friends from way back, folk I hadn't seen for years, some arriving from across the country, all requesting I embellish the inside covers with written terms of endearment. Strange what thoughts passed through my mind during the quieter moments.

I felt like an imposter, especially when someone asked me, "Well Eamon, what's it like being an author?"

The truth was I was really excited but from being a kid I was known as a good lad but one with not a lot between the ears. I did nothing to dispel these character descriptions. If anything, I contributed to them by some of my idiotic capers. It would take a bigger leap of faith than I possessed at this time. I assume quite a few folk were struggling with the same thought!

3.

A SECOND BOOK

Well might you ask! I thought long and hard before taking this decision. It came down to the folk of Bury and surrounding towns with their wonderful heartfelt comments finally convincing me how much enjoyment they derived from reading my book. Family and friends very kindly advised me early on of their enjoyment, but you would expect that. I must admit it felt so good walking into Waterstones and WH Smith and seeing my book on the shelf! Even now it still gives me a tingle. Being informed the book is still selling well leaves me speechless. Well nearly!

Two things were instrumental in my decision to write another book. Firstly, the fact that there were a couple of tales that for one reason or another were left out of the first book and secondly, the fact that I am approaching the 60th year of my life. Many things in our technology driven world are so different from the world my generation was born into, some good, some bad. I do not assume anyone will find my views any more interesting than the next fella. I live in hope. Please bear with me while I regale you (or bore you!) with several tales that were meant for my first book together with reflections and opinions that hopefully will interest you, the reader.

4.

LIFE'S DILEMMAS

"It was the best of times, it was the worst of times", the opening lines to Charles Dickens' *A Tale of Two Cities*. After reading these words, the thought came to me that this could be a fitting epitaph for most of the people I know. It is a natural progression that as we get older we seek wisdom in the written word, the utterings of the older and wiser and our own life experiences. All in the hope of becoming, for want of a better phrase 'an interesting person'. I don't mean in a vain way. It just seemed to me that the people I was in awe of seemed to be the owners of heads full of interesting things. Alas, as ever this isn't always the case. Some folk seem to possess a presence that furnishes them with the ability to attract people without uttering a word. Obviously we will not include here the majority of very attractive folk. Their attraction lies in a baser emotion. And by working hard to gather as much wisdom as one can, will it guarantee they become interesting folk? Of course not! Success depends on subtle gifts of timing, on when to, even if to, impart their pearls of wisdom in order to correct, inform, help or fetch about a fitting conclusion.

Listen to me going on with myself. I apologise if I am boring you, stay with me. I will try to redeem myself as we go along. Let me take you with me on my own personal journey of confronting life's highs and lows.

At fifty-nine years of age I can honestly say that for the last couple of years I have finally felt content in my own skin. To begin the journey, let me return to those troublesome times of my teens. Like most of my peers, my biggest hope was to be one of the gang, able to adapt comfortably into the awkward situations which would regularly arise, i.e. mates who, on learning of your supposedly secret crush on someone, promptly and loudly informing that person of the fact in your presence, leaving you squirming like a decapitated snake. The inevitable confrontations with the guys that for some reason don't like you and decide they want to fight you. What the hell do you do? Not being a natural fighter, and with a sincere hatred of confrontation, I would desperately try to come up with any compromise that would leave my dignity intact. Sadly, some folk don't leave you room for manoeuvre. Luckily for me, on these few occasions, mates usually stepped in and saved the day but not always! On those occasions I made my way home to lick my wounds and, on at least a couple of occasions, ended up at our local infirmary.

As a scrapper I made a good plumber. The only thing in my favour was that I knew for a small fella I possessed strong arms. If I could possibly get my opponent in a headlock then I stood a chance. My mate Brian Heys loves to remind me of an epic battle I had with one of our co-workers at the luggage firm we all worked at. Word spread the 'set to' was scheduled for finishing time on the grass verge at the back of the mill. My opponent and I made our way to the venue accompanied by a good quota of the workforce. I cannot tell you how nervous I was waiting for the fight to begin. The one thing that dominated my mind as we faced one another was to put all my initial energy into forcing a headlock on my opponent, hopefully resulting in those immortal words "I submit".

I decided rushing at him and catching him unawares would be a good plan. My opponent had other ideas! The flurry of punches, from which I actually saw stars, left me in a precarious state. My saving grace lay in what should have been his finishing punch, which landed on my forehead and which fortunately caused my opponent more problems than it caused me and his face contorted with obvious pain. I rushed at him and forced him to the floor with my arms securely round his neck. We stayed in that position for around half an hour! Initially a fist would somehow snake out and find my already bruised face but, as the time slowly passed and most of our audience left the scene muttering unflattering remarks, I sensed my opponent becoming less active and in the end completely docile. Unbelievably he had fallen asleep! After I woke him up we decided to call it a draw, which I thought was pretty big of me. Brian says it was the most boring fight in the history of man. I feel I must say at this time that these events were few and far between. That said, most of my mates and acquaintances accept that no matter what you do to avoid these frightening events some folk leave you no choice.

Thankfully these were the times when, even with the folk classed as beyond the pale, there existed an unwritten rule that if one of the combatants, either verbally or by a sign, made it plain they had had enough then that was honoured. I do not want to dwell too long on what some folk would consider a not very nice subject but alas this is part of life. Luckily a very small part.

Still in my teens and though the hormones in my young virile body were giving me many moments of concern, the world I was living in seemed full of mystery and promise, with so much waiting for me. Even at this naive age, like a sponge I would soak up all that I found interesting or, if not interesting, something that would come in useful in the creating of the fella I was hoping to become. An obvious question is why a seventeen-year-old kid would have any reason to look beyond the time he was in. I will try to enlighten you. From the time I was old enough to listen and largely understand what was being said and done around me I sensed when wisdom was being spoken. Like a moth to the flame, certain people attracted me. In this part of my life I was lucky in so much as there were enough of these folk to satisfy my thirst. Why the thirst existed in the first place, I know not.

Although I had friends, looking back I always felt the need to have a best mate. My best mate through school was a lad named Paddy, a lad of Irish descent as I was. Paddy, like me, was making his way through these formative years, sometimes stumbling but always progressing. I knew even then how lucky I was to have Paddy along to share thoughts I could only share in trusted company. Such a blessing!

There were kids I knew that for one reason or another were loners and, as a result, probably lonely. Though this saddened me, at this time in my life my empathy was never acted on. To be honest, our young minds were full of longing, fear, hope and a determination to enjoy this crazy game called life. The overriding thoughts passing through our teenage minds at this time, unsurprisingly, were all about girls. I confess I adored them, not just the ones I fancied, all of them. They fascinated me, the way they moved, smelled, spoke and thought, but mostly their mystery. I fell in love on a regular basis, luckily mostly unrequited. I say luckily because love affairs can have a devastating effect on your physical and mental health.

At the time of the inevitable break up, in nearly every case there is no quick fix. As in the case of a death, there has to be time to grieve. In my case the effects of these break-ups were so extreme I was unable to operate as a normal human being. Whilst I was feeling so desolate it seemed incredible that life was going on as normal around me. Alas I was unable or unwilling to take part. It seemed almost as if I became an actor on a film set, not sure what I was doing there or what part I was supposed to be playing. This must have been worrying and confusing for my family and close friends. People I knew seemed to be able to handle these stressful events without losing themselves. I realised then I had a problem. A problem that sadly would create havoc in my future relationships.

Strangely there was something about these painful times, something to do with the anguish they produced that sadly I was drawn to. This realisation worried me so much. I knew I was treating this part of my life too seriously. I lived in the hope that time would empower me with the answer. In fact it was a long time coming. God This sounds depressing!

Troublesome love life apart, there were decent lengths of time where I felt grand and enjoyed life to the full. Being a member of the Kavanagh clan and discovering the joy of reading were the mainstays of my sanity.

5.

WANDER LUST

At this stage of my life I lived in the company of my mum, dad and seven siblings and, although all from the same litter, we were as different as could be. This huge family resided in a big old Victorian house not far from the town centre. The town being the old mill town of Bury in Lancashire. Although large, our house in Oxford Street struggled to provide adequate sleeping room. Those were the days you just 'made do'. Sometimes it was hard to find any privacy but somehow we managed. We were a close family in every sense of the word.

My memories of our previous homes were vague to non-existent and the little knowledge I do have was passed on by my elders. After the war Mum, Dad and baby Mary settled into our first Bury home in Cecil Street on the Mosses. In the back passage to our home there was a row of old tumbler toilets, each one catering for four separate homes. Bet they could tell some tales. Our nextdoor neighbours, the Ellis family, consisted of mum, dad and thirteen kids. Apparently Mr Ellis only had to take his socks off. The modern view of this would be taken up with the frightening logistics. The old view was just to 'get on with it'.

Our family then moved to a brand new house on Primrose Drive on Topping Fold Estate. For some reason mum could not settle there, so with two further additions to the family, Patrick and Sheila, we made our way to 21 Avondale Avenue at the top of Hornby Street.

Our John, Margaret and myself came into the world while we resided there. Funny the things that stay through the passage of time. A magic tunnel! To locate this you needed to make your way down Victor Avenue on to Firssy woods. If you looked down this so called magic tunnel and squatted down, you could travel around fifteen yards to the other end where, after descending a couple of feet, you were greeted by the fearsome River Irwell.

The only other recollection I have is of the playground on the spare ground at the back of our house and of on one particular day being carried by Dad from the roundabout where I had fallen asleep after being sick. The only friend I remember from my time at Avondale Avenue is Paul Flemming. In future years he would become a fanatical Manchester City fan. Our Pat and the bigger boys would play footie near an old air-raid shelter at the far end of the spare ground.

One night the initials DM=SK appeared on the gable end wall of our house. Apparently young Derek McCarthy declared his love for our equally young Sheila. 'Young love'. Incredibly these initials, despite attempts to erase them, survive to this day.

Our next move was a strange one. By the way I feel I must state here that Mum and Dad were never in debt to anyone. This time we were heading for the Maskel Street, which literally ran up to the town's yard gates where Bury Council dumped the contents of their many bin wagons. As you can imagine, the local rodents were more than happy to share our small but weatherproof home. In fact so much so our cat, Posh, was putting in double shifts and still losing the battle. It was bad enough for us lads; I can only imagine what it was like for the girls. By this time Kathleen and Michael had joined our ranks. Just over the road on Todd Street lived another large Irish family, the O'Brien's, all bonny lasses, and good lads.

6.

ONE AND ONLY U.F.O.

Just arrived back home after spending just over an hour galloping round the running track on Market Street. Nothing unusual about that. I always had it in my head that these extra exertions might just give me the edge at a time when it mattered – the last quarter of a footie match, a time when fatigue tends to take its toll. I always preferred on these occasions to go solo. The fact I would be alone allowed me to concentrate on the task in hand without the pressure of social considerations.

It was a grand winter's night, a clear sky, so a little chilly, but dry. Plus when you're galloping round you end up mighty warm. So I am on my last lap and decide to give it my all. That last lap took everything I had. Hands on my hips, struggling to fill my oxygen starved lungs, I looked up to the heavens. I can only speak for myself but the sight of the moon and thousands of twinkling stars filled me with awe, similar to the feelings you get when standing on the shore of an ocean. Very humbling! Sorry, mumbling on again. Well as I stared at the sky towards Bury centre, with my back to the street lamps on Wellington Road, an object that seemed to consist of nothing but pure rich light appeared! What shocked me was the angle at which it arrived at its present position. It literally took my breath away by the way it shot from the stationary position it had held for around forty seconds to about half a mile above my head. The oval shaped object shot off diagonally at a speed that I had never seen the like of, bar a shooting star. For a moment I just froze, still staring in the direction of the object as it took its leave. Trying to collect my thoughts,

I looked around hoping to see any other person looking skyward. Sadly there was not a soul to be seen.

Typical! Who is going to believe me now? If I could have found someone else who had witnessed this event the story would have carried more credence and my inevitable doubts concerning my own senses would not be as acute. So do I now share this apparent revelation with my folks and risk the understandable jibes that would without doubt follow my impassioned tale. Upon remembering mum's enjoyment in relating stories of my youthful tall tales of snakes in the garden, and one particular whopper when I informed mum that the school had completely disappeared, I decided I would see what sort of mood the family were in and then take it from there.

It would have been around 8.30 pm when I walked through the door. As I passed the front room which served as mum and dad's bedroom/leisure room (a necessary arrangement simply due to pressure of numbers) they were just settling down with a brew and toast.

"Hi, I'm home" I said.

"Did you have a good run?" they replied.

"Yeah, I enjoyed it" I answered.

"When you have had a wash, make yourself a brew and relax," my mum said.

"Will do," I replied. I made my way through to our living room. My appearance hardly caused a ripple as all the other family members were engrossed in an episode of *The Beverley Hillbillies*, a family favourite, only just behind <u>Steptoe and Son</u> and *Kung Fu* with David Carradine.

As I dropped my kit bag to the floor the scene was the one where Mr Drysdale had collapsed and Miss Hathaway had fetched him round by waving money under his nose and said, "Wow, that was a bad one. It took a twenty dollar bill". Well, we all just cracked up.

Brilliant! Then I made a big mistake by uttering the most welcoming words to greet a Kavanagh's ears, "Anyone fancy a brew?"

Before I knew it I had seven cups lined up in front of me, trying to remember who wanted what.

After making the brews, I squeezed in between our Margaret and Kathleen and watched the rest of *The Beverley Hillbillies*. As the credits rolled I made my way to the kitchen. After putting my sweaty kit into the dirty wash basket, I made my way to our bathroom at the top of the stairs. As I felt a little drained from my exertions, I decided on a 'tinkers wash'. Anyone reading this with a hint of Irish blood running through their veins will recognise this term.

Although I felt ready for sleep, my mind was racing with what I had witnessed earlier. Sleep would evade me. May as well sit amongst the family and just try to gauge their mood. So I again squeezed in, this time between Kath and my younger brother Michael. At this time Michael and I were not close. Don't really understand why. I was only sure the problem lay with me. Suppose the thought of communal mates did not appeal to me. 'Time out' and all that. Being only three years younger than me, Michael was developing into quite a character. Good looking and intelligent, he left me in the block. Yes, almost definitely a little of the green eyed monster. Being the baby of the family and all that goes with that sealed his fate with me. Kathleen, on the other hand, well she is a darling and very protective of all her family.

"So, how was your run?"

"Different, you would not believe how different". Suddenly I had the attention of all my family members. Even Dad who was busy smoking fags almost as quick as he could roll them asked why. The time felt right so I related my tales as eloquently as I could. A few expected comments.

Pat asked, "have you been drinking?"

Sheila replied, "it would have been on a helicopter", and John just sat there with a gormless grin on his face. The others, Kath, Michael and Margaret stayed silent but their expressions betrayed disbelief.

This, sadly, would not be the only time when not one member of my family believed me. That should have been the end of the matter. Not for me. Oh no! The human mind, truly a God given gift, but in my case at this time was a curse and I lay in my bed wide awake all that night as my mind attempted to make sense of what had happened. Our John, my older brother, snored away in his bed. I came to the conclusion what I had seen, and I had seen it, was definitely not of this earth. That is ok you would think, a little frightening maybe but here I lay, a pretty good catholic boy, no matter how I looked at it, it just would not fit in with my beliefs. As you can guess, a sleepless night followed. Alas as dawn broke, still no answer. Shattered and frustrated I finally accepted I just had to let it go. Or better still; as in the Beatles song *let it be*.

Mum and Dad enjoying a drink at the Cotton Tree pub.

A few weeks later, a mate, Alan Dawber, called at our house and informed me that Tony Smith, who at this time ran a football team from the Kay Club on the Mosses, said we were to meet him later outside the club for a quick chat. Tony was not the easiest fella to let down and, as it was a Friday; there was no work the next day. So at around 9.30 pm Alan and me made our way to meet Tony. After a short discussion, Tony informed me all he wanted was for me to help him out now and then for important games for the 'Kay Club'. In their ranks at this time were two fellas I knew pretty well apart from Alan. One John Rawlinson and another real character, John O'Donnell who in later years committed an offence that right or wrong had many folk in Bury doubled up laughing their heads off. John, one day decided he wanted to steal a JCB, which he successfully did. Then unbeknown to anyone but himself he parked the said machine outside his home. It wasn't to prove the hardest case Bury Police had ever cracked. But John was a good footie player, as also were Mr Rawlinson, Mr Smith and my mate Alan and on the couple of occasions I played for them I enjoyed myself.

7.

DAD

If my old fella had a passion for anything apart from my mum and a pint of Guinness it was westerns. If he wasn't watching them, he was reading them and I have to admit his passion for westerns had a lasting effect on us Kavanagh males. It seems that if my three brothers and me had to choose our favourite type of film it would be a western. Truth be told, I reckon the majority of the lads from my generation held a subdued longing for the life of a cowboy, which is no great surprise as we spent many hours imitating them.

Dicky Bird estate was to our young minds a reasonable 'Wild West'. The place known to us as muddy mountains, which was to become the M66, was just about perfect with its collection of raised mounds which were perfect for us young cowboys to mount shoot outs. Once we had learned to make a 'berry gun' our excitement knew no bounds. It was so maddening when some folks would not stay dead when clearly they had been shot. Westerns were the only reason you would find us young ones exerting no energy; sat transfixed, watching our heroes living the life we so envied them for. I mean what is not to like? Mounting your horse, clicking your heels together and riding off into the sunset, rescuing fair maidens from 'no good sons of guns'. Accepting her words of appreciation and then bidding her farewell after explaining to her you needed to sleep under the stars, attend rodeos and simply could not be fenced in.

What a life! That sense of freedom would appeal to most menfolk. Oh to be a cowboy! Just you and your best friend, your loyal horse; never quite sure what would greet you in the next town or while out in the wide blue yonder, being on your guard for those pesky Indians. This was a time when men lived by the law of the gun. Law enforcement was at best, slight. The life of a Christian sheriff would almost certainly be a short one. Unless that sheriff was the one and only Wyatt Earp. The shootouts and scrapes this fella was involved in whilst incredibly never receiving so much as a graze from a stray bullet! He remains my all-time hero. Sorry again!

As I was saying, the days me, my brothers and dad sat transfixed watching a western on TV were without doubt special. Occasionally I would sneak a look at the others faces and had a good idea what they were thinking. At this time my favourites were *Cheyenne* with Clint Walker who started his working life as a nightclub bouncer. At six foot six inches he was made for this job. How he ended up as an actor I have no idea. Clint, for me, had it all for a cowboy star. Such a powerful presence it literally emitted from the TV screen. And that voice, to me the quintessential cowboy drawl.

John Wayne came a distant second to our Clint. We would never miss *Wagon Train*. Ward Bond was a natural leader of men, another brilliant role model for our receptive young minds. *Rawhide* starred my all-time favourite actor, the one and only Clint Eastwood. At this time he was a young raw actor learning his craft. I feel no embarrassment in admitting as the decades have passed, Clint has supplied me with some of the most magical and powerful emotions I have ever felt. It seems to me that as Clint gets older, just like a good bottle of wine, he just improves. He is best known for the spaghetti westerns. Fabulous deviations include, *Dirty Harry, Magnum Force* and, one of my favourite love stories, *Bridges of Madison County* with Meryl Streep.

In the *Flags of our Fathers*, Clint corrected a wrong done to a Pima Indian by the name of Ira Hayes. Ira was among the two hundred men of the American army who mounted an offensive against the

Japanese at Iwo Jima. He also was among the men who erected the American flag on the summit. He is depicted in the fabulous statue that graces Arlington Cemetery just outside Washington DC. Clint was determined to let the world know how this brave young Indian, who's valour was unquestioned, was let down by the Government who had so mistreated the folk of his nation. A truly great film. Yes, it seems Clint is as good a producer as he is an actor. *Grand Tarino* is such a feel good movie. I so enjoyed it. A glass of good red wine and a good film. Life does not get much better. Sorry again, must stop my mind drifting.

I sometimes pondered over why Dad loved westerns so much and I spent many an hour trying to imagine what his childhood would have been like. The only siblings of Dad's I got to know were his sister Frances who just resembled my dad in drag. Frances swore like a trooper but had a heart of gold. The other was Dad's brother, Michael, our lovely Uncle Mick. A gentle, softly spoken giant. Instinct told you that you could place your trust in any one of them, which is something, I consider precious. Hardship was an integral part of growing up for them as kids. By any standards they were poor. Then again, so were many Bury folk during the forties and fifties. It was the hard times they lived through that prepared them so well for the challenges of the future and when times became easier they fully appreciated it and never took it for granted. Dad once told me he was fourteen years old before he had his own pair of shoes. Before this time, he smilingly informed me, come Sunday, the Sabbath, he would polish his feet. I also wondered if Dad missed his homeland, and more to the point his kinfolk. I could never imagine living anywhere but Lancashire. Along with its shortcomings it has many more positives.

Lancashire folk represent the best qualities of what it means to be British. I could no doubt find a warmer, more picturesque place. All right for a holiday but even after just a couple of weeks I always look forward to returning to my Lancashire home. My best mate from my school days, Paddy Holmes, has now lived in Australia with his wife, Joan, for around thirty years. Paddy reckons the quality of his and his family's lives has been improved no end by their decision to emigrate. Daz Connray, Brian Green and Timmy Devault are other former Buryites who have followed in their footsteps.

To be fair, they all seem to be prospering and good on them. The only way I would have considered such a move would have been if it were possible for every member of my family and all my mates to join me. Somehow, apart from the fact I am too old, the logistics would have rendered it a fantasy. And believe it or not, I would definitely miss the rain. I know it sounds daft but I kid you not, on the few occasions I have found myself trapped within the borders of some mad hot country, by the end of the holiday I have found myself desperate to feel and hear the patter of rain on my skin. The lovely rain that will freshen the air and bring life to plant, animal and human alike.

8.

SATURDAY MORNINGS

I look back fondly on Saturday mornings during my days at St Gabriel's. After my breakfast of soft -boiled eggs and toast, and with a final check of my kitbag I'm off. Minutes later I was at the front door of our 'keeper and my mate, Edward Wrobleski. Eddie's house was round the corner on James Street facing Wood Street Mill, which at this time was our John's place of work. Eddie's Mum answered the door, I found Mrs Wrobleski's broken English with a strong Polish influence very endearing. The fact she was a darling helped I supposed. After enquiring about my folk's health, she set about preparing a light snack in order, in her words, "to give us wings". With me and Eddie sat at the small dining table next to the rear window, Mrs Wrobleski placed in front of each of us a small plate each containing two slices of Polish bread, thickly covered with liver pate. Gorgeous! Even though I would have already had my match day breakfast of two boiled eggs and soldiers, this was irresistible.

Eddie's old fella was okay, if a little stern. In later years Mrs Wrobleski would relate to me the amazing story of how she met her husband in a POW camp in Italy and amazed me with stories of the hardships they went through. Not once did she betray any bitterness. Sadness, yes, but that was all. After finishing our meal and thanking his mum, Eddie and me set off for the home of another of our teammates, Nello Oliviero, our star player.

The year before I had quizzed Nello on how his folk came to settle in Bury. He told me his mum and dad were living in a town named Avellino. One day a very smartly dressed English fellow arrived in the town and began approaching the young men of the town, informing them that he was organising a gathering in the town square for any men interested in working in England.

As you can imagine Avellino in the 1950s was a very rustic place and work for young men was scarce. Anyway Silvio attended the gathering where the smart English man held court. Those present were informed that if they decided to accept the chance of work in England, their passage would be paid for them. However if they decided to return to Italy before they completed three year's service they would have to pay back the cost of their passage. Silvio's mind was made up. He, his wife and three-year-old Nello set off for old Blighty. As it turned out, along with other menfolk from the town of Avellino, they found themselves working very hard for their pay at New Victoria Cotton Mill on Wellington Street. Silvio and his family, along with another Italian family, took up residence at a house on Belle Vue Terrace, off Manchester Road. The family, as time passed, were able to purchase their own home further down the terrace.

After mine and Eddie's arrival at Nello's home, his Mum would insist we sat down at their large dining table to partake of the Italian delicacy known as 'Pobs', which is basically lumps of Italian bread soaked in warm milk and a little sugar. Doesn't sound to appetising does it? But I kid you not, it was lovely. It's a wonder I was able to get a gallop up after this, but you will remember what we were like as kids, boundless energy and even more enthusiasm. I must have been playing really well at this time and was promoted to the Senior Eleven and joined the ranks that included Saint Gabriel's stars such as Daz Conray, Manuel Meleski, Leo Smith and Kenny Buggie. I cannot tell you how proud I was. Another lad who was promoted to the seniors (my year) was Mark Wilcox. He and his brother Gary (whose gorgeous sister Carol was arguably the bonniest lass in the school at that time) were great company in the Alfred Street days.

9.

AUNT RENIE AND MUM

Most Saturday afternoons I would arrive home to the sight of our Aunt Renie and Mum employed in endless conversations. Each in an armchair placed either side of a roaring fire (summer or winter), lovingly created by Dad. What always tickled me were Aunt Renie's legs. The heat from the fire afflicted them with a red mottled effect. For some reason Mum's legs escaped this less than attractive effect. As far as the two of them were concerned, these times were their times and the world stopped for them. They were to be kept watered, fed and ashtrays emptied at regular intervals. Supper would be left to one of the older girls to prepare. At this time, stews were the order of the day. When there are many to feed, it is simpler and easier. The girls would see to all the chores.

In Mum's view of the world, it was not manly for males to get involved with domestic chores. Having said that, me, Michael and John were allocated a small job each. Mine was making the fire each morning. On cold winter mornings I found this very testing. It also for some reason left me feeling good. John's contribution was to chop the wood for kindling. My memory denies me what role Michael played (probably overseeing me and John). Truth was my sisters' lives were without doubt a damn sight harder than ours.

10.

CHRISTMAS

As Christmas came around the feeling of excitement seemed to ooze from the very bricks and mortar of the Kavanagh house. We would all get caught up in the warm atmosphere, only improved by the raised spirits of all involved. Mum somehow weaved her magic. Our house in Oxford Street would be transformed by the enjoyable creation and hanging of homemade decorations. The house was large, but even so, how Mum kept our presents hidden from our prying eyes, I will never know. We were not kiddies anymore but even so the excitement never weakened.

On the day itself, after attending morning service at St Marie's, we would make slow progress home, crossing the Mosses then down Spring Street, exchanging greetings with every soul we passed. Within an hour of our return home, Mum with help from the girls, would have our dining room table groaning under the weight of the most gorgeous assortment of seasonal food. Mum never let us down. With meagre funds, she made sure every one of us ate like kings and queens. Along with our full bellies, the comfort contained in our strong family circle was bolstered by the 'feel good events'.

11.

ST GABRIEL'S

The following year was my, and many other kids, last at our school St Gabriel's. Daunting and exciting! Also few of us knew what lay in store for us. At this time I still lived with the dream of becoming a professional footballer. Along with many others I will come to accept that is all it ever was, a dream. The reality that beckoned for the majority would be factory work and manual labour. I cannot complain for truth be told, if you were determined, without doubt you would be given the chance to better yourself. There were so many factories and other places of work, no able bodied person would have any problem finding gainful employment. The thing was, there was so much going on around us we spent very little time pondering our futures in the big wide world. We simply lived in the moment, and left tomorrow to look after itself. On face value, not a bad strategy but it held its own drawbacks. Important decisions were made almost instantly and rarely properly considered, the results being sometimes less than favourable.

As with any large school, St Gabriel's was populated by all manner of mankind. Thankfully the majority by far were grand folk. A few not so grand, and a tiny few bordering on evil. The number of occasions I witnessed acts of outright cruelty were so rare they would never leave me. One of these rare acts of evil concerned my old mate Nicky Jones.

Nicky's family hailed from the Fairfield area of our town. Nicky's folk were similar to my own, in as much as in providing for their kids left no room for luxuries. One morning I was strolling along the dirt track that led from Manchester Road to St Gabriel's with my mucker Paddy Holmes. Our chat was interrupted by a sight that stopped us both in our tracks. Walking a couple of yards in front of us making his own way along this path, appeared to be the familiar figure of our mucker Nicky Jones.

What was so unfamiliar was the fact our mucker was attired in a 'fish tailed parka' if you don't mind.

"Cor blimey. Nicky who are you trying to impress?"

"No, no. It was my Christmas box from Mum and Dad. First time I have worn it".

"Your folks come into money then".

"I know, couldn't believe it neither, aint complaining".

We made our way to the cloakroom where Nicky hung the parka with a certain reverence. When dinner break came, as per usual a footy match would be arranged within our spacious playground, surrounded by open corridors leading to various classrooms. Once arranged the match would commence with the tenniser being chucked into the air usually accompanied by a shout of, "let battle commence".

The game had been going on for a while when my attention became focused on a verbal exchange between Nicky and one of the bullies our otherwise brilliant school had in its ranks. His name will remain anonymous to protect the guilty. This conversation ended with Nicky with tears in his eyes screaming angrily at the bully. Paddy and me arrived at Nicky's side as the smirking bully took his leave.

"Nicky. What's the matter? What's he said to you?"

It took a while for Nicky to calm down enough to inform Paddy and me what had passed. The bully had called him over and said, "Jonesie, you know your new parka, well it's a blazer now".

"Nothing for it, come on let's see if he was just winding you up".

We approached the cloakroom apprehensively in the knowledge this idiot was well capable of something this sick.

We hadn't even entered the cloakroom before the strong smell of burning material greeted our noses. As we entered the sight of the remaining remnants of Nicky's parka, basically the hood, was still smoking. Nicky for a while was inconsolable. Even the two coats hung either side of Nicky's hadn't escaped and were badly scorched.

"I swear, I will have him," he said.

"You won't be on your own Nicky," said a furious Paddy.

"Now hang on a minute you two, let's think this through".

I knew Paddy, knew he wouldn't hesitate to challenge the bully, but I also knew, even if Paddy was victorious, it wouldn't be the end of it.

"We need a plan. My mum and dad will go mad. Paddy, get your head working."

Almost straight away my freethinking mucker's eyes lit up.

"Nicky do you happen to know where your Mum and Dad bought your parka?"

Nicky named the large clothing store near the town centre. The three of us then entered into creating a plan to replace Nicky's ruined parka, which three catholic boys should never have been involved in.

Among our ranks at our school were a couple of fellas who, let's say, were skilled in the art of obtaining things illegally. Paddy advised one of these dubious chaps we needed a big favour. Before he would ask what was in it for him, Paddy reminded this chap how he had saved his worthless hide from two bullies not two weeks before. Reluctantly he agreed to join us in our mission. While Nicky waited outside, me, Paddy and 'Fingers' entered the store with as much calm as we could muster. Already briefed by Fingers, our jobs were to distract the attention of the two assistants whilst Fingers did his dastardly deed.

Carrying no bag but wearing an oversized coat, along with a description of the burnt parka, his aim to acquire the same or as near as damn. Well, I hesitate to sound proud but it speaks volumes that it was never mentioned again. Also three highly embarrassing confessions were made the same weekend. But poor Nicky was lost on how to thank us enough for what we did. He knew it went against all we believed. The new acquisition being a little tighter than the burnt parka, we told Nicky he could lose a few pounds.

12.

OUR NIGHTS

As I walked the small distance to the Kavanagh home, my face was furnished with a smile in the knowledge Saturday evening was 'our night'. Us kids were treated by Mum to sweets, crisps and pop, a once a week treat only. Whilst Dad and the older members of the family would be 'out on the town', Mum and the rest of us would arrange our huge sofa and chairs around the open fire. The curtains would then be pulled together to create a mood that Mum was aware would encourage chatter. To be fair to Mum she would answer any awkward questions honestly; us kids wanted to know the ins and outs of a cat's bottom. Well you know what I mean. Mum would not even 'sugar coat' the enquiries concerning her less than happy childhood. This had the effect of forcing our young minds to accept that not everyone in this wonderful world is 'nice'. Which, looking back, was no bad thing.

Us kids loved 'our nights'. The fact we would still be gathered round the fire until 10pm made us kids feel so privileged. As much as we dreaded Mum uttering the words 'up the dancers', we would never plead with Mum for more time (much as we would like to). Mum made sure we were all tucked up in bed before any of the adults arrived home. Mum would rather us kids did not see the effects a little alcohol had on folk who were normally ordinary, decent human beings. Or, in Dad and Pat's case, a lot of alcohol.

On rare occasions us kids would be woken by Mum giving Dad a hard time over the state he came home in. These would also be the rare occasions I disagreed with Mum. Dad's reputation as a true grafter among his workmates was legendary. Okay, Dad would have far too much to drink, but he was never aggressive. Truth was Dad, when drunk, was a pussycat. No, to a certain extent I reckoned these lively nights out with a few of his workmates around the town's Moorgate area, were a necessary release for a hard working family man.

13.

FAMILY SUNDAY

The next day, Sunday would see the Kavanagh's up early and attired in our Sunday best. We would walk the short distance to our church, St Marie's on Manchester Road, taking in Spring Street, which at this time housed one of the last Blacksmiths operating in the town. Horse traffic was not exactly heavy. Thankfully there seemed to be enough folk seeking to present this chap with various metallic tasks to keep him clothed and fed.

Passing through Moss Street I could not help marvelling at the fabulous stone carved figures gracing the upper reaches of the Art Gallery and Library. It always amazed me how some fella with a chisel could create an art form that, although subject to severe weather conditions, would last a thousand years.

"Eamon, are you coming or what?"

Once inside our church the rest of the family would take their seats before I sat down. I would make sure everyone had a prayer book. By the time my task was completed, I was lucky to find a seat with my family. More often I would be sat with strangers.

My biggest fear while knelt or sat in church was my failure to control what thoughts would invade my mind while in God's house. Now you will know the more you attempt to keep certain thoughts from entering what should be a mind containing only pure thoughts, you can guarantee the pesky little critters will somehow worm their way in. The times I have had to forgive myself for the impure thoughts that flounced like monkeys on a hot tin roof into my consciousness. Here I was in God's house with really naughty thoughts going through my mind. The turmoil in my besieged head resulted in physical responses in the form of hand wringing while little groans would escape from my throat. Unaware of the reactions of anyone near me, I was too focused on trying to bring my thoughts back to what was going on around me. In the end I came to accept I could never vet the thoughts before they trundled into my mind. However, as so often happens, once the fear receded then to a certain extent so did the problem.

After mass the family would make our way across the Mosses leading to Spring Street, across Heywood Street and home. Mum would waste no time in preparing our Sunday dinner. As a kid the effort needed for feeding nine hungry mouths was lost on me. After taking my turn to collect my dinner plate I would take a cushion, place it under my bottom and squeeze between my siblings on the floor.

If we were really lucky we all would be transfixed watching a grand Sunday matinee film. Chaos would ensure when, while watching the film the picture would vanish leaving a tiny white dot that would soon follow suit followed by shouts of "don't believe it", "God's sake. Who's got a tanner?" A sixpence would be inserted into the box and the catch turned and the picture resumed. Hopefully nothing too crucial was missed.

14.

ON THE HUNT FOR MUCKERS

Later I would set out in search of playmates. Bry Heys, my mucker, liked chilling in his room Sunday afternoons. Fair do's. Me and my pushbike – graced with the popular cow horns – headed for Alfred Street. As I approached the hardware shop on the crest of the railway bridge my attention was drawn to the old lady who ran the shop with her husband. Waving and shouting, obviously in some distress. I pulled over to see if I could help.

"Can I help?"

"Locked myself out, been visiting my hubby in Bury General and I have left a lamb joint on a low light in the oven!"

As the lady was talking I was already scanning the building for possible entry points. The only one I could find was a horizontal narrow window that was ajar. It would be a squeeze, but fortunately it was just to the side of the sturdy looking drainpipe. Revealing my plan to the lady, she looked a little doubtful.

"Don't worry I'm about eight stone wet through, it will be okay".

"If you're sure, don't want you getting hurt".

Reassuring her with the information I was very agile, my only worry was the fact I was wearing my 'new to me' Levi's. They fit me just grand.

So off I set, scaling the drainpipe in no time. Now the tricky part, tentatively stretching across, placing my foot on the narrow brick ledge, I eased across, one hand holding the bottom rim of the open window. Safely across, I forced the narrow top of the window as wide as possible.

"Here we go", hoisting myself head first through the narrow space. I found myself jammed by the protruding window latch. I could move neither forward nor back.

"Are you okay?" the lady asked.

"Yes, won't be long".

Below my top half was a chest of drawers. Luckily no ornaments adorned its top, just a fancy lace cover.

"Nothing for it, here goes".

To force the issue I jerked myself forward. I was sickened to hear the tearing sound emitting from my groin area, so much for my new Levi's. Shite! Well let's get the job done. Gently lowering myself onto the chest of drawers then made the short leap to the floor.

The room was obviously being used for storage. Boxes of all things sold in a hardware shop were stacked in every available space. There was an odour I was unable to identify in the room. Not offensive, just a little stale. Making my way down what was obviously the original staircase I was struck by the powerful smell of paraffin. Hardly surprising I reached the front door to be greeted by the sight of the key still on the inside of the door.

"There you go darling".

"Oh thank you so much".

"Oh my have you torn your pants?"

"No, no they were like that before," shite what can you do?

"Well listen let me give you something", opening her purse.

I said "No thanks, glad to help, see you soon".

She shouted after me. "Next time you come for your paraffin, you won't be paying for it".

"That's something. Mum has a paraffin heater in our bathroom, that will be grand". Quick trip home to change and put my Levi's to rest. Gutted! And off again down Alfred Street.

As I approached the junction with Killon Street, a few of the lads were sat on Harry's fence. Harry, Mick and Glen informed me they were up for a rat hunt on the banks of the Roach. The river lay just behind the huge Pilot Mill that dominated Alfred Street, a mere couple of hundred yards distance. I didn't fancy another trip home for my gun, so for this trip I would just be company for the others. As the four of us made the banks of the Roach by 'Gigg Paper Mill', we met up with another of our muckers, Alf Coop.

"How ya doin cocker?"

"Sound, yaself?"

"Grand. That's a nice looking bike you have there Eam. Fancy a swap?" Alf was holding an air rifle. It wasn't a BSA or a Webley, even so my love of air rifles was so strong.

Before I was fully aware I had already said, "Sure".

After shaking hands, Alf was off on my lovely bike. Well better check my new acquisition. I bent the barrel and loaded one of the pellets Alf had left me. Took aim at a tin can on the bank opposite, gently squeezed the trigger, to be greeted by a short metallic grinding sound. The pellet was spat from the end of the barrel to land with a pathetic plop in the water at my feet. It took a good while for intense laughter to subside along with gurgled remarks such as, "never mind Eam, you can use it as a club to beat the rats to death," followed by more laughter.

"There is only one rat I would like to beat to death with this useless gun. Only he has made off into the sunset on my lovely old bike".

The lads eventually agreed it was wrong of Alf to pull a stunt like that with a supposed mate.

Glen said, "I would ask for it back".

Mick chipped in, "they shook on it".

Harry added, "the thing is Eam, you should have at least checked the bloody thing before you agreed to swap. Treat it as one of life's lessons. Sometimes even supposed mates let you down. Come on let's get on with the hunt".

After a couple of hours we were beginning to have trouble remembering what a rat looked like, when who should we meet up with, but none other than Harry Owen, along with his legendary dog 'Rebel'. Story goes Rebel can sniff out a rat from 100 paces, even with a heavy cold. Now we were cooking on gas. Around twenty minutes later, just under the Seven Arches viaduct, we hit gold. There were rats everywhere. The lads' comments about using the rifle as a club came to pass. With Rebel seeing off at least four of the critters and me and the lads accounting for around twenty rats.

As we made our way slowly back, we decided to skirt round the field belonging to 'Water Farm'. Strictly speaking, you are supposed to ask for permission before working farmland. But hey, what the heck! Around half way round the perimeter of the field we decided to rest up for a fifteen-minute break.

As the light was slowly fading, I decided it was as good a time as any to relieve my swollen bladder. I had been peeing for a couple of seconds when Wham! A bolt of pain shot through my willy. With such power I was knocked to the floor. Not before I let out a blood curdling scream that frightened the lads to the point where a few of them were openly upset as they thought I had been shot. Instinctively I had unbuttoned my pants and was holding my painfully sore and bruised willy.

"What the bloody hell. What have you done? Got it caught in your zip?"

"I was just having a pee, when wallop. Cannot tell you how painful it is".

Mick asked, "where were you stood having your pee?"

"Just there, next to that fence".

"What, that electric fence?"

"What, it's electric. You are joking!"

"No you have peed on an electric fence".

"So what," I said, "I'm telling you now my willy never touched that fence".

"No but your wee did".

"So what?"

"Well," Mick said, "let me educate. Your electric current will travel through liquid".

Don't believe it, they are off again, like a pack of demented hyenas. Must admit even I found myself chuckling when Harry joked, "you will have to tell the doctor to take the pain away, but leave the swelling ha! ha!"

15.

14TH BIRTHDAY

As my fourteenth birthday approached my mate, Bry said to celebrate I had a choice. East Ward Youth Club or the roller-skating
capital of the north 'The Nevada' in Bolton. It was a tough one. I
really enjoyed our occasional trips to the youth club just off Bell
Lane, which was patronised by many of our muckers, Mick Green,
John Canterbury, Jackie Driver, Chris Brooks and Roy Horsefield
(Lang) to name a few. Then again the Nevada was a place we always
enjoyed. Usually the 23T bus from Kay Gardens was packed with
teenagers making the pilgrimage to the roller skating mecca. I never
really got the hang of roller-skating but was just good enough to get
by. In a way this made for more fun and was only awkward on the
rare occasions when a young lady would ask to join me for a holding
hands skate and I had to rely on the young lady to steady me.

Sadly I contracted a bad case of gastroenteritis. Misery was my
companion for a good two weeks. No school, no footy, no nothing.
During the day I was camped on our big sofa with Mum tending to
my every need. I would often drift into a deep sleep while watching
TV, never too long, as regular trips to the loo were required. When
the rest of the clan began arriving home gradually the sofa filled up
and I was gradually forced to the back of the sofa, unable to see the
TV, but at least I could join in with some of their chatter.

Kath would keep me up to pace with anything that went on at
school. My energy levels during this illness were very low. As a result
I was always drifting off along with the family's comforting voices.

The two weeks dragged on so slowly. I had very few visits from my muckers, as they were worried about contracting the illness. I could hardly blame them as it left you feeling so weak. As a normally very fit kid, these very rare bouts of illness I thought of as a curse but having Mum's undivided attention felt so good. She would occasionally impart just a little insight to her vast wisdom.

"Remember Eamon, happiness comes in little packets, not too often, but we have to appreciate them in whatever form they come. You will soon be feeling your strength return. Trust me, you will certainly feel grand then".

And of course Mum was right. One morning I woke with renewed strength in my forsaken body, it seemed to me after my long convalescence, my body felt refreshed and strong. This was a Friday, so I had the whole weekend to enjoy.

16.

EMBARRASSING HUNT

Saturday morning I was up early and out with Tina, my Jack Russell at my side and Percy, my ferret, up my jumper. With my rifle slung over my shoulder, I headed for the area known as 'Down Gigg'. Through this area ran the majestic River Roach, my destination. It felt so good just to be out in the fresh air. The cool autumn sun on my back seemed to enrich my already high energy levels. Making my way along the riverbank with Tina enjoying the concoction of smells greeting her sensitive nostrils and Percy's lack of movement informing me he was in a deep sleep, my body heat encouraging his slumber. No matter, I was content to follow Tina's lead, watching for signs of vigorous tail wagging.

Eventually we reached the banks of Goshen playing fields. At last I saw Tina with her head rammed into a small hole while wagging her tail. Brilliant! I felt almost guilty waking Percy from his slumber. Placing Percy near the entrance to the hole, I then took a step back, rifle at the ready. Tina, resembling a statue, so focused on proceedings was she, was ready to spring into action.

What happened next took us all by surprise. Percy for some reason seemed reluctant to make any progress down the dark tunnel and then unbelievably began slowly retreating from the tunnel's entrance. Oh My God. From the hole's entrance came into view the snarling head of a creature I had only seen once before. Once seen never forgotten! The creature this head belonged to, whilst not large, was similar in attitude to a 'Tasmanian Devil'. A weasel now confronted Percy, who happened to come from the same family, and seeming well aware of this fact, showed due respect.

Tina's ignorance of the fact was to bring chaos. At a speed the weasel made the bank top and set off across one of the several football pitches. This one to my horror had two competing football teams in the midst of a competitive match. Percy was snatched up and I raced to join Tina in the chase. The comical sight of a dog chasing a weasel and a kid holding a ferret chasing the dog and weasel was not lost on me. The ensuing commotion fetched the match to an abrupt stop. Along with cheers from the captivated audience, Tina made a lunge at the weasel's rear end, sending the weasel hurtling through the air. The weasel landed face to face with Tina.

As Tina made to inflict the fatal bite, the weasel's sheer speed enabled it to inflict a vicious bite to Tina's sensitive nose. Tina let out a piercing yelp and, shaking her head vigorously, sent the weasel on another aerial trip. Instead of once more taking up the chase, Tina made her way forlornly to my side. The shook up weasel made a speedy dash for the welcoming riverbank. As me, Tina and Percy made our way across the football field, from the players and referee came appreciative applause, which in turn brought an involuntary smile to my face.

That evening sat with all the family members, I related this story and we all ended up enjoying a good laugh. All the while Mum was tending to Tina's badly gashed nose.

17.

FIRST JOB AND FIRST PINT

After a short unpaid sabbatical, I joined the workforce of local luggage firm Antlers on Alfred Street. The work was mundane, and the pay poor. But for the first time in my short life I walked through Antlers gates at the end my second week with my wage packet in my back pocket containing £5,17s 6d. Better still, family history told me my first wage packet would be all mine. After that a third would go into Mum's purse for the good of the whole family. This fact made me feel like a proper grown up.

While still enjoying the novelty of earning a living, me and my mate Bry Heys decided to try our hands at purchasing our first pint of beer. This really excited me and worried me in equal measure. The two of us were well under age for drinking alcohol. I informed Bry that I had heard the Brickcroft Tavern or The Star on Freetown tended to be relaxed concerning young drinkers.

Bry dismissed this, "look Eam, if we are going to succeed, it needs to be a local pub."

I couldn't argue with his logic.

So early evening one Friday, the two of us set off in our glad rags for The Roach Pub on Rochdale Road facing the park. Sneaky looks at Bry's face told me this mission held no fear for this confident lad. On the other hand, as we neared our goal yours truly was beside himself with self-doubt. As we approached the entrance I took Bry by the arm and whispered, "cannot do it Bry, not yet anyway".

"Eam what is the problem, the worst thing is they refuse us. What you worried about?"

I struggled to put up a decent argument. "Just give me a little time Bry. I will be ok."

As we walked along Pine Street we passed the home of an aged lady who was a neighbour in our Dickybird days. Elsie was a wild old soul. As I have confessed many times, old folk have a calming effect on me. Naturally it took some coaxing to get Bry to agree to me having a little while with Elsie.

The only snag being Bry said he would wait for me in the Roach.

"What do you mean, I will have to meet you in there?"

"God Eam, you are supposed to be grown up now remember."

"All right see you in there, won't be long".

Elsie opened her door on my fourth knock. "Well, look who it is. What do I owe this nice surprise to?"

Entering Elsie's dimly lit, cosy living room and thankfully realising Elsie was alone I related my sorry tail. Elsie explained while unsure of the wisdom of seeking to patronise public houses at my impressionable age, it was hardly unheard of. She then told me of her eldest son Paul's similar situation. Paul, like me, looked even younger than his tender age. His problem was lessened by his older sister's interventions. In a delicate operation, the small amount of down or 'bum fluff' that occupied Paul's upper lip, was skilfully coated with his sister's black eyeliner. You can probably guess what followed.

After hugging Elsie and thanking her for her efforts, I set off a little reassured in the direction of the Roach Pub. Deep breath at the door, then made my way past the bar and entered the main room where I picked out Bry in conversation with an older couple. After my call of "Bry" it seemed that I had silenced all conversation in the room. For a second, maybe two, there was complete silence. The bellowed words "Heil Hitler" were followed by howls of laughter.

"What the bloody hell?"

Folk actually had tears running down their faces. I quickly vacated the Roach along with the knowledge it would be a long time before I could live this down.

Bry caught me up as I reached Pimhole Road. I could tell by the way he could do nothing for laughing I had really done it this time.

"What the bloody hell made you blacken your lip, God's sake Eam, she didn't do a very good job. Come here".

Bry, using the sleeve of his shirt and a bit of spit, removed the offending mascara, which I thought was pretty good of him.

"Well what's the plan now"?

Bry glanced over at the Peel Hotel. The stare held doubt.

"Come on, we will try the Crown". Bry obviously was unsure of my chances. He had already sampled his first pint, which he reckoned tasted like nectar. His only problem was his baby faced mucker.

"Well what the hell. Can it get any worse"?

On the way into the Crown Bry whispered, "You go sit down, I will get us a couple of pints".

Looking round nervously, hoping not to see anyone I knew, I took a seat next to several elderly gentlemen. My thinking was that the older generation were very tolerant of behaviour they deemed understandable. This paid off. These chaps sensed my nervousness and their gentle quips calmed me some. Bry made his way to join me with two lovely looking pints of bitter and took his place at my side. He wasted no time in striking up a conversation with the old chaps. This felt good. Me and my mucker enjoying drinks with these local gentlemen. Alas, however perfection is an elusive state.

A good hour passed in genuine enjoyment. Okay, not totally relaxed, regular checks on folk entering the snug 'just in case'. Eventually a lad we knew only as Mick arrived. Summed up by most folk who had met him as a 'wide boy' and a 'big mouth'. Our eyes met and he must have seen the plea in eyes for him on this occasion to just do the decent thing and keep his gob shut.

"What the bloody hell! Don't tell me they are serving milk in here now".

The instant this lovely fella took a seat still laughing, the shadow of Bry stood over him. I have no idea what Bry whispered in Mick's ear, but no more jibes came my way.

Well, apart from the fallout from the Rochdale Road debacle, I set out on a lasting love affair with the pleasures of meeting in public houses with good folk, where the alcohol itself seemed just a complementary addition.

18.

THE GROG

Like most young lads of my generation, I enjoyed a drink, and as a result, not too often, but a couple of times I have ended up in some weary states. I had mates who I never saw in a drunken state probably because they were afraid of losing control or simply hated the inevitable aftermath. That was their choice and I always respected that.

There were a couple of occasions I certainly wish I had had a little more self-control. One Saturday night in 1977 for some reason I had drunk myself into a drunken stupor. The night had started well enough. Me and my mate, Bry Heys had started out in our local, the Peel on Rochdale Road. After a couple of pints of Guinness, Bry said "why don't we have a pint with your old fella?"

Early on a Saturday night Dad would be found in the Nags Head just off the Rock, near Moorgate. It was also known as 'Little Ireland' because for some reason it was a magnet for folk from the Emerald Isle. Dad was really pleased to see the two of us. Dad insisted Bry and me sit down while he got us, as he put it, "a pint of porter". I was a little embarrassed as Dad told all and sundry that his son Eamon was rejected by Manchester City, and, without doubt, it will forever be their biggest mistake. Handshakes all round, very hard to look proud under these circumstances.

One of the fellas sat with Dad was a chap named Tommy Kelly. As I worked with Tommy's wife Alsa, I was already acquainted with Tommy and I really liked the man. We left the Nags Head and made our way to the Cotton Tree. Whilst Bry got chatting to a couple of our muckers, I heard someone call my name. I looked round and looked into the lovely face of Theresa Wosser. For a while if felt as if there was only me and Theresa in the pub. I must confess, I so fancied this girl. The thing was, at this time I was seeing a girl called Pat from Walnut Avenue. Pat had recently split with her fella, a bloke called George, who worked as a bouncer at Rebecca's nightclub where Pat waited on.

As I was chatting with Theresa, I had to keep reminding myself that I had arranged to meet Pat later that night in Rebecca's where she would be waiting on. As Bry was married to his lovely wife Hazel, he would head home after last orders. Bry knew my plans for later. As a result he kept glancing over to where me and Theresa were stood and as my eyes met his, he slowly shook his head. We are just chatting I mouthed. Truth was, I just wanted to stay chatting with Theresa all night. Bry, hand on my shoulder, said, "come on Eam, we are off to the Blue Bell". Reluctantly I left Theresa to take her seat back with her folks. As I left we caught each other's eye. So much promise was held in those split seconds. Well, you know when something just holds so much promise. Right or wrong?

In the Blue Bell we met up with a couple of lads I played footie against, Ste Deakin and Mick Turter. Both Ste and Mick always seemed to me to have a bit of the devil in them. Good lads, just real pranksters. Ste and Mick suggested we have a little contest. They wanted to see who could down a pint the quickest. Best of all, as it was their idea they would stand us the drinks.

When they came back from the bar pints were placed in front of each of us.

"Well", said Ste "on the count of three. 1, 2, 3".

I decided to adopt a slow but steady swallow and closed my eyes to help me concentrate. As the last drop of the harsh tasting pint of bitter went down (not my usual tipple), I placed my glass on my beer mat and opened my eyes to see the other lads had all finished before me. My first words were "who won?"

"Your mucker Bry".

Bry looked rather flushed but pleased nonetheless.

"What sort of bitter is that?" I asked.

"Enriched," said Mick. This comment tickled both Mick and Ste.

"Right" said Mick, "catch you boys later. We are off ta! Jockey".

Didn't know about Bry, but my head was spinning.

"All right Bry?" I asked.

"To be honest Eam, I feel a bit rough. Won't be a mo," he replied.

I made my way to the bar, picked out the girl who had served our friends their pints. "Excuse me, those four pints of bitter you served about 10 minutes ago, were they just bitter?" I asked.

She replied, "two of them were, the other two had treble whiskeys in them."

"Oh God Bry, it's no wonder we are both feeling rough. Them buggers laced our drinks with whiskey".

"Ya joking," Bry said, "let's get some fresh air. Don't have to tell you the effect that had"

Bry said. "I'm away home Eam. Think you should do the same cocker."

"I can't. I said I would meet Pat, it's our first date, sort of."

Bry slapped me on the back and set off down Wash Lane.

The next part of this story had to be filled in by my old mate Big Mick Suthurst, as I had no recollection. Mick informed me that his attention – along with about fifteen other folk queuing outside Rebecca's – was taken by a fella holding up some drunken bloke towards the entrance. A couple of yards short, he lowered the guy to the floor saying, "told you I would help you to get here. Good luck," which fetched laughter from the bored crowd.

The guy then proceeded to crawl on all fours to the entrance and it was then Mick noticed the clown on the floor was me. Mick made his way to the front and pulled me to my feet and asked the bouncer (Pat's ex) if I could come in? George's reply; well let's just say it wasn't very nice. Mick, being the bloke he is, carried me to the taxi rank and told the driver where to take me. The rest of the night is a complete blank.

In the hours of Sunday morning I was woken from my drunken slumber by someone tugging at the ends of my trousers. After a bit of a struggle my trousers were off. Next I was pulled into a sitting position and came face to face with Pat's smiling face. My shirt and vest were removed and we both collapsed into each other's arms. It felt lovely but because of the condition I was in, I was asleep in minutes.

The next morning, Mum made her way up the stairs to my room with a cup of tea to be met by a confusing sight. I was lay on my back asleep with both my arms outside the covers. What confused Mum was the sight of another arm across my neck. What happened next, I could never understand, and if you knew my mum, you would struggle as well. Mum woke me and softly asked the young lady's name.

"This is Pat Mum".

"OK, when you are ready make your way downstairs," she said.

"Oh my!" I said to Pat. "This ain't gonna be easy".

"Your Mum seems sound," she replied.

"Truth is Pat, I cannot believe how well she has taken this".

Nothing for it, me and Pat got dressed and very sheepishly made our way downstairs to join the others. As me and Pat entered our living room, all eyes were upon us. Not a word from anyone. A short awkward silence was broken by Mum announcing "Eamon took ill last night and Pat was kind enough to fetch him home". Still silence, but the expressions on my sibling's faces spoke a thousand words.

Me and Pat took shelter in the kitchen, then in the yard. Family members kept passing the window, which looked onto the yard, sneaking glimpses of the dirty two. I had my own questions to ask Pat. "How did you find our house let alone my bedroom?"

Thankfully now I had my own room. Pat said George had told her what had transpired and she searched out a lad she knew who also knew me. He told her my address and that the house's nickname was the Chapel, as the front door was never locked. As to which room I would be in, he couldn't help her.

"So, how did you find my room?" I asked her.

"Well, I found your left shoe on the landing and your other shoe halfway down the inner hallway leading to your room," she replied.

"Cor, blimey" I said laughing, "you would make a bloody good burglar".

Pat said she had had a few drinks herself and was determined to make sure I was okay. A kiss seemed in order. I can safely say Pat and me enjoyed our short time together. She even came to watch me a couple of times when I was playing for Elton Fold. I only have fond memories of the girl.

19.

TWO WEEKS IN TORQUAY

The following year, a friend Dave Cowley, who lived on Spring Street, asked me if I fancied a couple of weeks in Devon, the Babbacombe area of Torquay to be exact. Dave informed me I would be staying with his auntie. As a result I would only need to find my fare and a bit of spending money. Too good an opportunity to turn down, one lovely mid-July afternoon saw me and Dave arrive in the centre of Torquay after a very long coach journey. We then took a taxi to his Auntie Anne's home. The house turned out to be a comfortable mid-terrace. After a decent cup of tea and introductory chat, Anne showed me to my small but airy room, which had a high ceiling and what looked like the original dado rail.

After putting away my few belongings I made my way downstairs to join Dave and his auntie again. Then to my extreme surprise, Dave announced he was off. He said he would be back for me within the hour. I was dropped on. Going off Anne's reaction, she knew of this arrangement. Well, no use bothering now. Will seek Dave's explanation later.

As the weather was grand I decided to go up to my room and change into shorts, Tshirt and pumps. True to his word, Dave returned, dressed in similar clothes to myself. On grilling Dave about this strange arrangement, his answer was that as his Auntie Anne had only three bedrooms, one for herself and one for her son, Keith, this left just the one for me. Guess you are thinking the same as me. I put it to him, his answer was, he wanted company, so it was only right that he should soak up any extra cost. Well to be honest

I found this fair enough. I am not going to try and cover two weeks events here, so here is the very short version. It turned out Dave's generosity leaned more to personal gain.

On that first outing to see the sights we just happened to meet up with a bonny local lass already known to Dave from his several previous visits to his Auntie's. Rather than play gooseberry to the lovebirds, I made my excuses and left them to enjoy each other's company. The next morning, I was up early, breakfast eaten and out the door for a day on the beach, trunks on beneath my shorts and a beach towel under my arm. A small amount of change saw me take the cable car that lowered me down to Babbacombe beach.

I now realised my first mistake. Babbacombe beach was made up of large pebbles and, just before the water line, shale that so tickled my very sensitive feet. With just a towel there was no way I could get comfy so I purchased a raffia mat from the beach shop. Now I was in business, mat down, towel on top. Grand! As the sun beat down, I drifted off and, after an erratic night's sleep, I slipped easily into oblivion.

I was awoken from my slumber by the sound of girls giggling. Yes, as I feared, they were looking in my direction. Looking down at myself, my whole body had taken on a red glow. I decided to sooth my reddening skin by going for a short swim. As I rose to my feet, the two girls went off on another laughing fit.

To be fair, I must have looked a sight. My front was beetroot red, my back milky white. There was a huge rock around 150 yards out from shore, which I decided to head for. Now I was not a good swimmer. I got my little experience from the baths on St Mary's Place, off Silver Street. I waded slowly into the gentle waves, going deeper as the shale beneath my feet sloped downwards. God, it felt good. As I took the plunge, my whole body cooled instantly. Instinct told me, this would do me good. Adopting the crawl style (said to be less taxing), I set out in the direction of the rock. After a couple of minutes I am thinking, is it me, or is that damn rock drifting away from me?

By this time I was tiring quickly. A decision had to be made, and quickly. Coming to my senses, I about turned. As I made the turn, I felt something wet and slimy grab at my flailing feet. Second mistake, I ducked under the water to get a view of what it could be. Oh my god! Strands of giant kelp were lapping all around my feet. The roots of these giant plants were concealed by the sheer depths they rose from. Panic shot through my trembling body. As I broke the surface I let out an involuntary scream for help. I could find no cohesion from my limbs, again I found myself under water.

The fact I could not see the bottom terrified me more than I could say. The ghostly waving kelp just increased my terror. Was this to be the end? I am not being dramatic. The huge arms of kelp lapping around my tired body seemed determined to coax me into a watery grave. As I went under for the third time and I feared the last time, I held my breath and closed my eyes tight shut.

As the moment when my lungs would scream to be filled again neared, my salty tears mingled with the salty water. I accepted this must be my time. God had other plans for me. At the exact moment my mouth opened, and with the last of my strength I kicked to the surface in the hope of one last lung full of oxygen. As I broke surface, I felt powerful arms pulling me upwards. I was so thankful to be able to breathe freely.

"How you doing son?"

I could only grunt, "OK".

By the time we reached the beach, I was in a really emotional state. Escorted to my towel and clothes, I kept telling this wonderful chap how thankful I was. He might not have known it, but I knew without him I would be, as they say, swimming with the fishes. I convinced my hero I was okay and needed no medical help. As we parted I asked his name.

"Tom, Tom Clancy".

Even in the still fragile state I was in his name brought a smile to my face.

People had been gathering round me, asking was I okay. The last two spectators were the two girls who had been laughing at me earlier. Obviously foreign, I struggled to understand their broken English. In their own way they were trying to apologise for laughing at the, to be fair, comical figure I cut. To the girl's credit, I gathered they were offering to see me home. As the still very strong sun was becoming unbearable, I declined the girls' offer – reluctantly – as they were lovely, and said goodbye and hoped to see them again. I then made my way back to Anne's as quickly as possible, while attempting to keep as much in the shade as possible.

As I was almost hugging the wall as I went along, I almost bowled over an old chap as I rounded a corner.

He stopped and said to me, "God son, you have burnt yourself badly there. Now listen, anywhere you can find it, gather a good bundle of nettles. If you have no gloves, use your T-shirt and when you get home boil it in a pan with some water. When it cools, dab it all over the burnt areas with cotton wool or a clean cloth."

After thanking the chap, I thought anything that helps me I am up for. As luck would have it, one of the hedgerows on the way home had plenty of fresh nettles growing beneath them. For this task my beach towel sufficed well enough.

On reaching Anne's, I explained what the old chap had told me. To my delight Anne agreed it was a tried and tested local remedy. So after what seemed a lifetime, Anne brought out into her yard a bowl containing the dark green soapy liquid. Although she volunteered, I decided it would be better for me to administer the liquid myself. As the burnt skin reached my intimate parts, it just would not be right. Thirty minutes later, job done. The burnt areas of my body were coated with what I hoped would be healing green slime. I stayed sat in Anne's enclosed yard for at least three hours, time enough for the slime to do its stuff. Anne ensured I was fed and watered during this time, after which I washed in a cool bath.

Making my way downstairs, washed with clean, soft clothes on, I felt 'mighty fine'. Strangely something told me not to disclose my little episode to Anne. As me and Anne sat watching TV, there came a knock at her door.

On rising, Anne said, "that will be Keith".

He had been visiting a friend in Exeter. So in no time at all I was shaking hands with Anne's son Keith.

"Nice to meet you."

No reply. No hug or kiss for his Mum. In silence Keith and his overnight bag made their way to his room.

"Is he okay?" I asked Anne.

"He is just shy, don't worry he is like that with everyone," she replied.

Takes all sorts, I thought.

As that night wore on, half way through a film I think was *In The Heat of the Night* with Sydney Poitier, Anne rose and bid me good night. So there I was enjoying this grand film, when the living room door opened and in walked Keith. No greeting, he just sat down to my left on the chair his Mum had a little while before vacated. I did not know how to react. Keith was a big lad, also a lad who held no interest in fashion. Practical would be the word. Not a hint of flamboyance. His mop of dark unruly hair seemed at odds with his conservative clothing.

"What religion are you?"

This opening line took me completely by surprise. I mumbled my answer, "Roman Catholic".

"Why does your religion forbid birth control eh eh? Insisting their priests stay celibate all their lives!"

I was dropped on. What a bloody question to ask someone on a first conversation. I was completely out of my comfort zone here.

"Don't mean to be ignorant Keith, do you mind if I just watch the rest of this film, it's brilliant".

Keith just got up and left the room, for which I was thankful. Strange fella.

The next day I felt so much better. The nettle mixture had worked. I just had to make sure I stayed out of the sun for a couple of days. Luckily there were plenty of walks with dense tree cover over the downs and beyond. I ran into Dave and the young lady a couple of times. I was polite, even though I thought him a let down. He asked me to join them the following day. I declined and said I had arranged to meet a girl. You know how it is, first date and all that. Catch you later. Another one for my next confessional.

The day before we were due to leave, I was wandering round the shopping area in Babbacombe, just checking out the shops, hoping to find something Mum might like. As I was leaving a gift shop with a nice decorative picture frame, I passed a young lad holding what looked like a small snake.

"Where did you get it?" I asked.

"Oh there are plenty in the woods hereabouts. They hide under piles of leaves or under fallen branches."

Brilliant!

"By the way they are called slow worms, they are really legless lizards".

Look like snakes to me. "See ya".

As I had my duffle bag with me, my mind was made up. I set off for the woods. It wasn't long before I was traipsing in the under-growth in search of a slow worm, legless lizard, whatever! All I knew was I wanted to get one back home. I could really have some fun with a little snake.

I searched and searched, no joy. I was about to give up when I spied a pretty large log. I knew I would have to be quick. I positioned myself, legs akimbo to one side. The plan was to flip the log over and just hope it covered a slow worm. Here we go! Over went the log, Bingo! Not one but two of the little critters. Before they could slither off, I held both in my hands; they went straight into my duffel bag. I headed off to hide my booty in the wardrobe in my room. As I had no idea what a slow worm ate, I stooped down and grabbed a handful of soil and foliage in the hope there would be something in there they could munch on.

On my arrival back at Anne's, I secreted the duffel bag in the corner of the wardrobe, remembering to tightly pull the strings together and wrap the excess around its neck. That evening I took a walk round the downs. Hoping I could meet someone, anyone, just to have a chat with. This had been a pretty lonely holiday for a chap who enjoys the company of his fellow man. I can safely say I have never been so starved of human interaction. It wasn't all bad news. This part of Devon had a big impact on me. It had lovely areas of natural beauty and was so clean. I was taken with the thatched cottages, lovely! This place would see me again and again in the future.

The morning of our departure I was up early. Anne had made an effort with a full English, which I so enjoyed. Next thing Dave was at Anne's door with a waiting taxi. I hadn't even packed my bag. I excused myself, legged it up to my room threw everything in my small Antler suitcase, then I remembered the snakes. Blimey! Come on Eamon. Get a wriggle on! I snatched up the duffel bag, checked inside, with Dave shouting up the stairs. "Come on Eam". Don't believe it, they're not there. I thrust my hand in and ran it round the inside. Gone! Where I can only guess. No time to ponder, case zipped up. A last hopeful look and down the stairs. A genuine thank you to Anne for putting me up. She cut a sad figure in my mind, few friends and had a strange fella for a son.

The long journey home was a little strained as Dave went on about what a great time he had had. Some folk! Also I prayed Anne was not afraid of snakes.

I had enjoyed the beauty of Devon, but as in future excursions to interesting holiday spots, I always felt good when returning to my hometown. After my Devon trip, I felt sorry for family and mates alike. Just wanted to chat, chat, chat. Reckon a bit of solitude is healthy. I had just had a bit too much.

20.

THE MAGIC VALLEY

Early one hot summer Friday evening in 1974 I found myself and a half a dozen of the Alfred Street gang making our way on foot up Castle Hill Road. Our destination 'The Magic Valley'; Deeply Vale. Deeply Vale in future years would be the venue for several free concerts that would attract thousands of folks keen to enjoy the brilliant atmosphere. Dave Kirsopp, a local lad was one to entertain the appreciative crowd.

As we made our way up Castle Hill Road, the gang seemed in good spirits. Glen said to no one in particular, "what we gonna do when we get up there?"

Almost in unison Harry and Mick replied, "We're on a magic mushroom hunt".

Me and a couple of the others asked, "Why?"

Harry went on to explain these small mushrooms contained a drug that changed optical and mental views of your environment.

Mick added, "Lewis Carroll, the author of *Alice in Wonderland* was using the rarer red variety with white spots. The ones he used in his pictures and I tell you now they are pretty damn potent".

Looking around at the others faces, I sensed a certain amount of doubt. Not just me then. As the weather was very warm, most of the gang had on just a T-shirt and jeans including Sandra and Sue. Now I realised why Harry was taking a duffel bag. Glen was wearing his denim jacket. He must have been roasting.

"Take your jacket off Glen, you must be roasting". As Glen seemed reluctant, I didn't push it. Half way past Walmersley Golf Club, the girls suggested we take a break.

As no one was against it, we settled down on the low perimeter wall. The girls were complaining they were thirsty. These were the days for some reason; even on long hot treks we never carried either food or drink. Tended to rely on nature's bounty.

Harry said, "look, there are a couple of springs and streams we will be passing, and you can drink your fill then."

"No way I'm drinking from a dirty stream," said Sue.

Harry's reply was, "running water is pure, but it's up to you".

Glen asked if we could search for some blackberries, wimberries, even crab apples. I must admit I was pretty peckish. Happily we found bushes overflowing with ripe fruit and the babbling waters of a stream stemmed our thirst.

It seemed Sue's thirst overruled her disdain, as down on her knees, hands cupped, she drank her fill. Finally we were back on track. As the day cooled, we turned onto Croston Close Road.

Harry's words, "we're nearly there," certainly pleased our ears. Especially the three of us who were Deeply Vale newcomers. As it turned out we still had a fair walk before we arrived at the Vale. Speaking for myself I was well impressed. Included in the pleasing vista that greeted us were rocky outcrops, ruins of old mills and a vast expanse of inviting grassland. Lovely!

As soon as we arrived Harry opened his duffel bag and pulled out half a dozen plastic bags to be used for our magic mushroom collecting. We were instructed by the well informed Harry and Mick to only pick the little button mushrooms that are crowned with what they described as a little nipple. So off we went in every direction, agreeing to meet up in around half an hour, at the spot we had just left. Didn't know how the others were doing, but the little blighters were providing pretty elusive. To be honest my heart wasn't in it. For one thing, there was no way I would be trying these little fungi that contained God knows what. No way. Another was, I was more interested in the ancient rocks, ruins and wildlife hereabouts.

After ten minutes I came across a lapwing's nest containing three speckled eggs. The mother of these eggs was making a bit of a din about thirty feet above my head. As I watched her descent, she landed a couple of yards from where I was stood over her nest. What happened next was a surprise, but not a big one. She began moving around, dragging her left wing that was extended. She was attempting to lure me away from her nest by pretending her wing was broken. Unbelievable. Now I had heard of this behaviour before, but this was the first time I had witnessed it. How clever is that. Experts would explain this as instinct. Well what does that mean? The same term is used for the little birds like the swallow or house martin. These tiny creatures travel thousands of miles from Africa, unbelievably to the exact same spot year in, year out. Instinct does not explain anything. Sorry!

Anyway I left the stressed bird to cover her eggs with her warm body. I decided I had better see if I could find any of the illusive mushrooms. The shouts I had heard from the others told me they were doing okay with their task. Later, as we gathered to display our bounty, along with the excited talk a voice of reason made itself heard.

Glen said, "better we don't try these out here, miles away from anywhere. Let's wait until tomorrow night. We will make our way to Inspiration Point down Gigg". To my surprise everyone agreed.

As it was still warm it was decided we would make our way to the quarries at Birtle near the Church Inn. These quarries were partly flooded, in places quite deeply. Once before more or less these same people had spent an enjoyable evening there. No reason today should be any different. As we passed the Church Inn, a few of the regulars were sat outside enjoying the view over the lake.

After settling ourselves on the rocks overlooking an inviting, what was called a 'lagoon'; Harry and Mick busied themselves rolling a reefer. Most of the gang enjoyed the weed. At this time it was considered harmless. As it was passed around, it was passed to me by Harry who said, "I know you don't smoke, but one drag won't hurt you".

Well what do you do? Copying Harry, who I had seen take a long hard pull, I did the same. Big mistake. It literally blew my head off. Head spinning, I made my way out of view of the gang to throw up the contents of my stomach, mostly half-digested blackberries. Feeling not right well really.

I rejoined the gang, some of them laughing at my ashen appearance. Then Mick jumped up. "Right, who's up for swim?" He then stripped to his less than pristine trolleys. Well, you can guess the rest. Just left yours truly on the rocks watching my mates having a real giggle, frolicking about in our own lagoon.

Sue shouted to me to see if I could find some bits of wood to make a fire. "We will need it when we get out".

"No prob that I can do," I replied.

I set off. Deciding to ignore the passing thought of hiding the gang's clothes it wasn't long before I had collected a good bundle of branches and twigs. After depositing my load, I set out and came back with even more. My next task was to find some tinder, all I could come up with was some wool gathered off the barbed wire that the sheep had brushed up against and a few dry leaves. I set about setting the fire. After building it up nicely, I borrowed Mick's matches and within minutes I had given life to a grand crackling fire.

As the lads got out of their soaking undies Sandra and Sue did the same out of our sight. With said underwear decorating the rocks above our heads, catching the last of the sun's rays we all sat round and the girls began singing the Beatle's song *Let it Be*. Not being a Beatles fan, but conceding they did some mighty fine records, I joined in. Sadly my voice added nothing to the quality of our communal effort. I kept it low. By doing so, I didn't spoil what sounded a pretty good effort by my gifted friends.

This musical treat carried on well past the last of the sunlight. Our acapella versions of classic songs like the Small Faces *Itchycoo Park*. Credence Clearwater's *Bad Moon Rising* and the Byrds *Mr Tambourine Man* were several that received an airing from 'The Alfred Street Choir'.

Again, I was sent to gather some more wood, this time in the company of Sandra. Our task was more difficult by the fading light. We managed somehow. Plus our sneaky snog I so enjoyed. So with our fire blazing away the talk turned to 'life after death' and if there was any or not. This is a subject that has always fascinated me. As a practicing Catholic, it would have been wrong of me to say anything that did not justify my weekly confessional trips to Father Fitzgerald at St Marie's. Mick's comment that confession was a fire ladder for Catholics caused more than a titter.

21.

TROUBLESOME REVELATION

The girls said that because they believed in ghosts, and Sue having seen one, it marked them down as believers. Mick, Harry and Glen all agreed death was not the end but they couldn't agree on what form it took. Someone suggested reincarnation but doubt remained about what form this would take.

What took place next was to be a pivotal event in my life and sadly not a beneficial one. The event I will shortly describe to you may seem on face value inconsequential, but for some reason it was to have an adverse effect on my life for more years than I care to remember. As Sandra stared up into the star-studded night and uttered the words, "I wonder where it all ends?" We all turned our eyes towards the heavens.

Mick answered Sandra's question with the answer, "it has no end. Infinity has no end."

Then Harry picked up a small stone from the ground at his feet. He held the stone above his head, held at the tips of his fingers. "Right" said Harry, "all I ask is that you imagine this stone travels in a perfect line for eternity, never needing refuelling. Where would it end?"

Glen declared very clearly, "back here".

By now I am hanging on Harry's every word.

Sue said, "It would keep travelling in an ever decreasing circle".

Harry said, "No it would never end".

"Nagh." I said. My mind since childhood had been assured there is always a beginning and an end. Common sense demanded it. "Nagh, Harry you're wrong".

"Listen carefully Eamon. This stone travels in a laser beam line, unobstructed by any stars or planets, it will carry on for eternity. Where do you think it will end? The nearest thing we have to nothing is a vacuum. This little stone could travel through a vacuum". Harry pointed to the heavens. "Out there lies infinity Eamon. You don't have to be clever to grasp that".

As we got our things together for the trek home, the gang were in high spirits, except me.

"You all right Eamon?"

"Yeah, yeah, I'm okay," I lied.

It was a long walk home. As we reached Oxford Street I bid farewell to the rest of the gang.

"You joining us tomorrow at the Point?"

"Yeah, see you tomorrow".

Sandra shouted, "don't forget," and smiled at me.

"I won't," I said.

There was no sleep for me that night, or for quite a few nights after that. Our John kept moaning I was disturbing his rest and kept waking him up with my restless fidgeting. I would wake up sweating, looking around the dark room, unable to come to terms with this knowledge I now held. Why it was having such a terrible effect on my peace of mind I could not say. To me it made a mockery of any logic I held. I felt like a small boat with no anchor on a stormy sea. The thing was, I knew Harry was right. How could there be an end. The fact was I knew there could be no beginning and this fact terrified me.

No matter how I tried, my mind could not come to terms with infinity. I knew I had to find some peace. I needed to function. It wasn't like I could just take a few weeks out to sort my head out. At last I made a decision that for now to put it out of my mind calmed my mind enough to get a couple of hours sleep.

After my day at Antlers spent in a robotic state and work colleagues asking, "are you okay Eamon?"

I said, "Well actually I'm struggling with being informed there is no end or beginning to the universe".

Could you imagine? Instinctively I headed in the direction of one of the terraced houses on Alfred Street that ran between Oxford Street and Wilson Street. The house I was heading for belonged to an old sage who actually fought in the Great War. Now approaching ninety, Jack Taylor still possessed an abundance of wisdom and knowledge that I intermittently needed. Not wanted; needed. Certain older folk attracted me because of their calming effect. No matter how troubled your mind, once in the company of an old sage, I guarantee you will leave their company a whole lot calmer.

"How are ya son? Come in, I'll put the kettle on". As Jack came back into his living room with two mugs of tea he asked, "What's the matter lad? Sit down why don't ya! Now I know something's up. In ya own time lad, when you're ready".

I slowly went through what had passed at the Birtle quarry. Jack just stared at me. It was a little while before he spoke.

"This may sound a little comical, but think of yourself as a little fish in a pond. The little fish doesn't concern itself with the outside world. The pond is its world. It's the same with you lad. What are you spending mental energy for on something that should have no impact on your life?"

I just sat there staring at Jack. Deep down I knew Jack was making sense. I just didn't feel it was what I needed to hear.

To me at that time, it seemed to ignore the issue. Basically I put it to the back of my mind. Now I don't know about you, but personally speaking, I find tucking anything away in a dark corner of your mind creates, if you like, a tumour that over time festers then creates real problems.

It was obvious even then there would be no easy answer, if any.

Looking back this inability to give complete closure to this, what I recognised as an illogical problem, manifested itself in the form of me needing to create intense emotional situations. Always with the people I should have been protecting, my partners through the following years. I came from a family where there was stability and plenty of love, which made this reaction even stranger. I would create situations, which would put immense stress on my shell-shocked partner, putting the relationship under terrible pressure. This in turn forced my partner into outbursts of emotional pleading. Obviously I was getting something from these energy sapping cruel events. God, this sounds so bad! For unfathomable reasons, these events made me feel awful, 'but alive'. To everyone else I was a 'great lad', I felt such a charlatan. As time passed things improved. Not fast enough to rescue a long-term relationship. I hereby thank the people involved so much. The three of them are lovely people who were deserving of a decent partner or husband, but incredibly still treat me with respect for which I will always be thankful.

Now I have revealed myself as a former basket case, I won't hold it against you if you close this book now. But please don't. Even with my flawed character, life was at times very rich. I just tended not to look up at the heavens much. Ha! Ha!

22.

NOT TOUGH ENOUGH

As time passed, I found myself playing in the ranks of the Huntley FC Team, playing at this time in the Manchester League. Strangely half the team was made up of Mancunians who took great delight in making fun of our Bury way of speaking.

"Eeh lad, how are thee".

"Is tha going up t'hill"?

With the onset of shortened daylight on training nights cars would be positioned to throw light onto the old doctor's pitch, enabling us players to practice the finer arts of the beautiful game.

Set pieces, or tuning of personal skills, were helped along by our Manager, Roy Freeman, aided by the one and only Tommy Allen. A very special man, Tommy probably would not have been conscious of the beneficial effect he had on me in my hope of maturing into a decent bloke. The revelation, brought about by my mucker Harry Chadwick, was not too far off. Sadly this would have a damaging effect on my fragile mental state. It was not long before my closeness to my brother Pat would be sorely tested. The team he played for, Tottington St Anne's, were playing behind the Rostron Arms at Edenfield. All I know is the weather was cruel. Hard driving, freezing rain. Three quarters of the way through the game, I reached the point where I honestly thought my survival was in question. After going past the point of caring about the upset I would cause, I shouted through the stinging rain over to Pat. "Pat."

"What?"

"I'm going off".

"Ya what?"

"I'm going off".

Then promptly made my way off the pitch, Pat's shouts ringing in my ears, "don't you dare leave us short now".

I felt terrible. Truth was I couldn't feel my feet or fingers. To me this was about survival. I know that sounds melodramatic, but I kid you not, I was genuinely worried. As I reached the sanctuary of the hut, I got out of my soaking kit as fast as my numb fingers allowed. Alas my bootlaces were to remain tied. My frozen fingers proved useless for this task. Desperate to remove my footy boots, I shouted to one of the hardy souls watching what remained of the game and asked if he would help me remove my boots. After unsuccessfully attempting to pull them off, he then began untying the muddy laces. I thanked him and set about drying myself off with my lovely big rough bath towel. As I dressed slowly, the feeling slowly came back to my extremities.

After ten minutes, I cannot tell you how good I began to feel. Euphoria flooded by grateful body. Don't think I have ever felt stronger. Strangely at this time it seemed unbelievable that I had just let my team-mates down because of a bit of rough weather. Fact was I had, and now my tougher team-mates began to make their weary way into the hut I still occupied.

What to do? Guess I should say something.

"Sorry fellas, just froze up".

Some of the lads were less than impressed. A couple made fair-minded remarks.

Then Pat came in. "Well, well it's our hero. Tell you now, you won't play for St Anne's again".

One of the other lads came to my defence. "Hang on a minute Pat. Eamon doesn't play for us normally. He was good enough to help us out and remember the only game we have won this season was when your kid scored two cracking goals against Totty United.

"You should be glad he is willing to lower his standards and help us out. And you have got to admit Pat, today's weather was pretty severe."

I looked across and mouthed a thank you for his words. On the drive back home Pat ignored me, which I expected. Thankfully it was not too long before normality was restored.

23.

PUSHING FRIENDSHIP

Sometimes when we were at a loose end, me and my mate Anthony Henry took a trip to Bury to Colson's Cafe. Anthony was a mad Leeds fan. He thought Don Revie was a God. He also supported his hometown. During the week many Bury players met at Colson's as well as parading round Kay Gardens. There was one time me and Anthony were sat upstairs enjoying our pie, chips and peas in this upstairs room, among other regulars were sat John Murray, Gregg Farrell and Peter Farrell. Anthony and me were trying to listen in to their conversations. (To hear what footy players talked about). There was some guy sat between us and our heroes talking really loudly, trying to impress the lads. He mentioned his own name several times, not normal in everyday life. Anyway he made it impossible to hear anything but him.

We were just about to leave when an old chap named Tom, who for a while served time at Antlers, entered the room. It didn't feel right to just say, "hello, goodbye," so Anthony and me ordered another brew while Tom had something on a muffin. Naturally he asked about the lads and girls who were his co-workers.

"Yes, Sid's still there, John Massey, John Read, Agnes McCarthy and Pat Hosker".

"They are all in good form".

"In rude health, all of them," I replied.

"Has his Royal Highness, Plenderlief ever graced you with this presence on the shop floor?"

"Only at Christmas time".

I then informed Tom I had recently left Antlers in favour of a position with Scapa Yarns at the back of Brewer's Arms pub facing Hoyles Park.

"How you finding it?" he asked.

"Life as a ring spinner is bloody hard Tom. Well if you're not going to stick to it, make sure you have another job lined up". Wise words.

The three of us were having a good old chat when into the room walked one Mr Timmy Devault. Timmy at this time was living with his Mum and Dad who ran the Clarence pub on the corner of Silver Street and Bolton Street. I noticed straight away Timmy's right hand was bandaged. He made his way to the table where Peter Farrell was sat with a couple of his team-mates. Their connection was the fact Peter was courting Timmy's gorgeous sister Dee. Through Timmy's raised voice the story of his blooded hand was revealed. Timmy had had a big bust up with his Mum and in temper he had punched a mirror. The outcome being the mirror was shattered and Timmy was left with a badly gashed hand. He had literally just got back from Bury General. The good news, no ligament damage. A couple of the Bury players had playful digs.

"Will you ever play the piano again?"

"That's the end of your sex life for a while".

As he turned he caught sight of me. "Hi Eam, suppose you got most of that".

"Yeah I reckon". Timmy, after nodding to Tom and Anthony, asked if he could have a quiet word. So I followed Timmy out into the street outside. Timmy put his hand on my shoulder he stared into my eyes and said, "Listen Eam. I know it's a lot to ask, but could you put me up at yours, just for a couple of days until I can sort something?"

For a few seconds I just stared at him. What the bloody hell! Myself and my first wife Jackie had a house on Raby Street, just off Bond Street. "Timmy let me have a chat with Jackie. Suppose we could bring Lee, our son into our room for a couple of days."

Truth was, I really liked Timmy. "Look, come round tonight, cannot see any problem with Jackie. She knows you well enough".

"Tell you what Eam, you're a proper mate." Timmy then gave me a hug.

Three months later Timmy was still in residence. After my 2–10 shift I opened the door with my key.

"Hi Eam, you okay?"

"Yeah, are you?" Straight away I could see Timmy had been crying.

"Where's Jackie?"

"Think she's in the kitchen."

"Right". I walked through to our kitchen. Jackie was sat at the small table we used for our meals. Her body language told me she was upset. Talking loudly enough for Timmy to hear I asked, "Well, what's gone on between you two?"

It was then I noticed the large box of chocolates on the worktop. Pointing I said, "Whose are these?"

Timmy then joined us, "I got them Eam. I didn't mean to, but I upset Jackie."

"Looks like you upset yourself too".

"You know me Eam, hate falling out with mates. Listen Eam get yourself comfy, I'll whip to the chippy."

After asking what we wanted he was off. I was thankful for the time to question Jackie. "Well what was that all about"?

"Trust me on this Eamon, he upset me. I realise now he didn't mean to. Don't make it anything it's not." Some of you will be surprised to know that is exactly what I did. Yes I know it seems naive. Truth was, as a mate, I liked Timmy. I had no problem living with the worst scenario. So while doubt remained, Jackie and me just got on with it.

Timmy, to his credit left our home but I can honestly say I found his company a joy. The only time I had a go at Timmy was when he was living down Gigg Lane with a girl called Janet. After knocking on his door, it was answered by a naked Timmy.

"Have I come at an awkward time haha?"

"No I was just gonna have a quick shower".

At the same time Janet was having a go at Timmy for answering the door in the nude. There is no way he would have been cold. A couple of times I had told Timmy "you could be the missing link". Fact was, Timmy was the hairiest fella I had ever known.

After his shower the two of us set off along with one of his golf clubs and a couple of balls to the large green area in Bury Cemetery. After inserting a tee, he placed the ball on the tee. As Timmy took the classic golfer stance, "hang on a minute Timmy". To our left, around a hundred yards away, there had obviously just been a committal. Folk were stood around the still unfilled grave. "Now Timmy, you make sure you keep that ball away from those grieving people".

"I play golf Eam, I know what I'm doing."

"Make sure you do."

Again, he struck the stance. A couple of ghost swings. Then "whack". Don't believe it! The bloody ball, travelling at great speed, was on target to land among the mourners. Unable to look, I stood in front of Timmy and screamed in his face. "Get over there and apologise to them poor folk NOW".

Sheepishly Timmy made his way to the probably shaken, but hopefully not hurt folk. I heard a couple of raised voices. Well it was the least he deserved.

The really sad expression as he returned calmed my anger instantly. "God's sake Tim".

"I know! I know, I have apologised".

"Well okay, let's go yours and have a brew Timmy".

If you could keep him serious long enough, and believe me it wasn't easy, he was a bloody good footy player. A real class act. But his real gift lay in the way he enriched any social gatherings with his unmistakable Devault Grin.

24.

ME, BRY AND MUSIC

One Saturday afternoon, after turning out with the first eleven, the really gifted characters that made up the 4th year, first eleven St Gabriel's footy team, I could hardly contain myself as I got changed into our brilliant blue and white kit. Just walking out with those boys felt so good. After getting home and getting some dinner down me, I set off for my mate Bry's house on Heywood Street. Mrs Heys answered the door and informed me I would find Brian in his attic bedroom at the top of the stairs.

"Ta Mrs H, I'll get up there."

As I made my way along the corridor that led to Bry's room, the door to my left opened and out stepped Bry's gorgeous sister, Delores, attired only in her bra and knickers. Here was a dilemma. Delores had not noticed my presence. Do I cough, or say "hi" to let her know I was there. As she made her way along, I decided to allow her to make her way uninterrupted. I reckoned this was pretty thoughtful of me. (I know what you are thinking). Have to admit took me a while to wrench this vision of Delores from my memory.

On opening Bry's bedroom door I was warned immediately by Bry to be careful where I was walking as many of his records were scattered over his bedroom floor. As I settled myself on the floor to one side of my mate, Bry said, "anything you fancy Eam?"

"To be honest Bry, not sure why, I fancy some Bowie".

"Well you're in luck, just bought this".

He then proceeded to take a single from a box of 45's, place the single onto the deck, then carefully lift the arm containing the stylus over the outer edge of the now spinning record and deftly lowering it onto the groove. The first few seconds were taken up with a noise similar to a distant plane engine. Then came the intro to Bowie's fabulous *Diamond Dogs* track. In unison me and Bry added our vocals to Mr Bowie's (as they pulled you out of the oxygen tent you asked for the latest party). Brilliant! We spent around three hours picking out records we fancied singing along with. Think we finished off with a track we both loved Joe South *(The Games People Play)*. Good powerful song.

As we had decided we had sung enough for one day, just for something to relax and listen to, Bry put the *album San Quentin* by Johnny Cash on the turntable. Halfway through Delores knocked on Bry's bedroom door. "It's only me boys".

"Come in", said Bry. In she walked carrying a tray with tea and toast. "Please marry me Delores".

"Eam, you all right".

"Oh sorry, was miles away in prison with Johnny" I lied. It was just too soon after my earlier encounter with the almost naked Delores for my overactive imagination to allow everyday thoughts.

"What you two up to tonight?"

"Thought we would get up Rocky Road – Crown, Peel, Roach then back to Peel for last orders".

"What about you Delores" I asked.

"I'm meeting someone later outside the Vic in Heywood".

Just for a second I think I hated this person. I know, very sad. "Well I had better start getting ready".

Before I could stop myself, the words flew out "need any help?"

Luckily Delores just laughed. Cannot say the same for Bry, just a look that said, "get it out your head".

"Catch you later".

"Yeah, have a good night".

In truth I knew Delores would never seriously take me on but there is no harm in having a flirt.

25.

INTRODUCTION TO DECEIT

Arriving home from work I enter the establishment known as the Kavanagh home. Hi ya to no one in particular. Around half of the family were present. Mum weaving her magic in the kitchen.

"Just gonna get changed," I shouted and went up to the room I shared with my older brother John. A quick change into jeans, T-shirt and pumps. Ready for the streets after finishing my tea, it's "see you later" and out into the wild beyond. Well, the area known as Pimhole anyway. As there were no mobile phones, the norm at these times was to just roam around and see who was on the streets or call at the house of a mucker.

On this occasion I had not been on the streets long, when I met up with my mate Paul Driver. "Hi Paul, how you doing?" I asked.

"Sound, you?" he replied.

"Sound". Paul looked more than sound. Attired in what looked like a new pair of fringed black royals, a nice fitting pair of faded Wranglers topped off with a white Tshirt and denim shirt.

"You on a promise?" I asked.

"Nah, just thought I would go touting the coffin dodgers for some work," he replied.

Although I doubted the sincerity of Paul's answer, the practice of knocking on older residents' doors, seeking work in the form of odd jobs was something Paul and me had adopted to furnish us with a little pocket money.

"You fancy some company?" I asked. As I turned to leave, couldn't keep the wry smile from appearing on my face and betraying my thoughts. The smile began to fade as I decided to track Paul. I was so curious as to what he was up to. I began to follow him, keeping a decent distance between us, to reveal if my suspicions were founded.

In this way we travelled down through the area off James Street that ran along Wood Street Mill. We went past the allotments, on up by the pig farm and then right onto the dirt track that took you to the "One Arch". As Paul passed through the entrance to the Arch, I decided to scale the bank of the arch that carried the Bury-Heywood line. This proved a good move. Under cover I made the short descent to the other end of the arch. The top of its facade rose around three feet above the ground I stood on. I was now twenty-five foot above where Paul stood lighting a fag, leaning on the rails of the small wooden bridge that spanned the narrow stream that ran the short distance to join its big cousin the "River Roach". Luckily for me, a small thorn bush allowed me to observe Paul with little chance of being spotted.

Paul's body language told me he was in a nervous state. After finishing his fag, he immediately lit another. Not normally nervous, or a heavy smoker, my interest intensified as to the identity of the young lady he was almost surely waiting to meet. But why the mystery? We were mates; he could have said, "I'm meeting a lass". He knows I would never ruin his chances by stalking him. I'm only here now because Paul obviously fibbed about what he was up to. Another ten minutes and a third fag later, Paul threw what was left of his fag into the stream below his feet, like it was toxic. Arm raised in greeting he shouted, "all right?" along with a big smile. I could vaguely hear a female voice answering Paul. Her identity concealed by the hill to my right.

By this time I was almost beside myself with curiosity as to the young lady's identity. Well my curiosity was soon quenched. The young lady now embracing my mate Paul was no other than the girl I assumed was my girlfriend at the time, Angela Owen from Cornwall Drive. To say this upset me would be one hell of an understatement. Outrage, jealousy, but the overriding emotion was anger. My first taste of betrayal left me literally shaking with pent up emotions, bursting for expression.

After their embrace, they slowly made their way up the hill to my left known as "Inspiration Point". My first instinct was to follow them, knowing there was only one reason a lad took a lass up to the Point. We will not need to explain here. Should I wait for them to be in a situation that allowed no argument from them? No, don't think I could handle that. A considered mature view would almost definitely be to leave be. Well, I was young and immature and frankly too damn angry to leave it. With my heart thumping in my chest, I tracked my faithless friends to a wooded area, just before the "Seven Arches". I concealed myself behind a young elder tree. I always liked elder trees. Strange why this seems significant. Considering the situation, who knows? At the moment I knew I could stand no more, I made my way to where they lay. Being so wrapped up in each other they were completely unaware of my presence.

"Alright you two?" I asked.

Paul pulled away like a thief caught in the act. For her part, Angela looked like a rabbit caught in a car's headlights. For a moment the three of us held our places silently. It was left to me to utter the time honoured words, "How could you?" Still nothing from them. "Nothing to say, or what?" My so-called mate and my loyal girlfriend.

"Oh, come on Eam, we have been seeing each other a few weeks".

"Well hang on, on the couple of occasions I have asked you to meet me, you have had something on".

"I understand you are angry, but don't make out we had anything special".

Paul finally spoke. "Listen Eam, I really am sorry mate, no excuses. When you said you were thinking of asking Angela out, I was gutted. I have always fancied her, just never had the bottle to ask her out."

Well he soon get over his shyness.

"Listen, the other week, the day of Angela's birthday, when you told her you couldn't see her, but would see her the next day. Well Angela was upset".

"Don't tell me you were there to comfort her?" I asked.

"Yes Eam, I was," he answered.

"Next you will tell me neither of you planned any of this."

"We didn't," said Paul.

"Right, like I believe you".

Angela turned round and said, "to be honest Eamon I don't give a damn whether you believe us or not".

I just stood there staring at them both. I suppose I was enjoying their discomfort at my presence. "Well I hope you will be very happy".

"God's sake Eamon, don't be so dramatic".

"Oh I'm sorry Angela for being upset; it's not every day you catch your girlfriend cheating on you with your mucker".

"Look it's like Paul said, none of this was planned. Circumstances. We are not proud of what we have done, but it wasn't like me and you were a devoted couple and a bit of advice for you. Next time you are with someone you really like, treat them a damn sight better than you have treated me."

I just stood there staring at Angela. To be fair, she had a point. I could feel my anger reluctantly ebbing away. "Well anyway I will leave you to finish what you were about to start".

"I know you won't believe me Eam, but nothing has gone on between me and Angela but I cannot say it wouldn't have if you hadn't appeared. Truth is we have only kissed. If you and Ange think you can make a go of it, I will step aside".

"What", Angela and me uttered that word in unison.

"I will be in Rocky Road Park. You two have a chat". And with that Paul walked off, leaving Angela and me in uncomfortable silence.

It was me who broke the silence, "well that was pretty big of him".

"Yes, it was. He's not like you Eamon, he's really shy. He was a nervous wreck when he told me he had always liked me. I am not bothered what you think; it was me who kissed him as much for him as myself. I will be honest with you Eamon; I know Paul will never let me down. He is the steady sort, might miss the drama a little, but not much. Don't look so sad Eamon; you know you will be okay. Your pride has been dented, it will soon mend. Now you can walk me to the park".

Angela began to walk off. "Well, come on".

In a dreamlike state I took my place at her side. We made our way along the top of the point, heading for the "One Arch". After descending the point, we entered the semi darkness of the arch. The words left my mouth involuntary. "What would you be doing now if I hadn't come along? Shagging?"

Obviously Angela's filter wasn't working either. We both cracked up laughing. The two of us had to stop walking, hands on our thighs, unable to breath properly.

So the two of us made our way to Rocky Road Park. We were still laughing as we approached Paul who was sat on the large polished rock at the side of the tennis courts. His body language revealed he feared the worst. I took a position facing Paul.

"Well Paul, I hate to admit it, but Ange has spoken a lot of sense tonight, so I am not going to be a mard arse. The main reason being I don't want to lose either of you as friends".

Paul shook my outstretched hand and repeated "friends". And with that I bid the two of them farewell and made my way home. My mind naturally kept wandering back to what had passed this crazy day. Badly needed the loan of an old sages ear, what I really needed was reassuring.

26.

REFLECTING ON LIFE

And that's how it was with Jack. Knowing that with what had passed this day my chances of having a decent sleep were remote at best. No, a trip to my own personal wise man was just the ticket.

"Come in young un. To what do I owe the pleasure"?

"Seeking your opinion Jack".

"Oh right. You make yourself comfy whilst I make a brew". Magic! Jack's home was sparsely furnished with old bits of teak furniture, a couple of yellowed photos of Jack's only sibling Mary who passed away a decade before and his best mucker 'gentleman Jim Booth' whose picture I sometimes noticed Jack staring at forlornly.

Jack's face lit up when talking about Jim. Jim had only recently passed on so I left it to Jack to recount their many escapades. The fact a picture of Jack's beloved wife, Linda was absent Jack explained by saying, "Bedside table lad. Her's is the last face I see each night and the first when I wake in the morning". I loved the smell of Jack's home. At a guess I would say a mixture of furniture polish and Dettol, which Jack swore by.

To be honest by the time Jack returned with two steaming pots of tea, I already felt calm.

"Now young un, in your own time."

So for the next half hour or so I relayed to Jack the events of the previous few hours. Jack never interrupted me, just listened patiently as I imparted my tale of woe. When I had finished, Jack stayed silent for a while.

Along with a developing smile, Jack said "well lad, there is chances for you yet. Given the situation you found yourself in, you showed maturity beyond your years"

"Do you think so Jack?"

"I do lad. What's more, because you showed maturity and forgiveness you have not lost two friends, who as we speak must be thinking you are a pretty "special fella".

This last comment of Jack's really lifted me. I suppose this was Jack's gift. After a while we fell into a comfy silence as we both stared into the flickering embers of Jack's coal fire. As had often happened before Jack's forlorn gaze fell on the old photo of his mucker Jim.

"Reckon you were very fond of Jim, eh Jack".

"I loved the man, lad".

"Tell me about him Jack".

"Only if you want me to. I will tell thee lad".

Jack carried on staring into the fire's dying flames as he began the tale of his and Jim's friendship. As they were born within weeks of each other on the same street off Bolton Road West, there is no mystery as to their introduction. They became close quickly. Many folk assumed they were brothers. Jack admits their likeness was striking, giving fuel to small town rumours. Looking back Jack reckons life for himself and Jim was a struggle, very spartan, the upside being for a few years their imaginations and enthusiasm enriched what could have been a somewhat dull life.

Our young heroes could be seen on their summer expeditions in places such as Strongstry village, down Chatterton Lane, Irwell Vale, Turn Village and of course the moors over Holcombe, but mostly they tended to tread the banks of the Irwell. On a whim they would enter wholeheartedly into a game of hide and seek and, incredibly, sometimes taking hours to trace one another. Sometimes they took Jim's dog, Sammi, a lurcher cross. After a hard day's hunt, to the delight of their families, they would return with a brace of rabbits.

Jack explained his and Jim's life received a rude awakening when they began their jobs together.

The mill for the lads meant long hard hours for very little reward. And, what drove them both mad was that they spent most of those lovely long summer days in dull, airless rooms with very loud machinery. It seems no mystery that when war came in 1914 our heroes were only too happy to volunteer for one of the regiments up the valley. They were both excited at the thought of escaping the hard mundane toil of the mill and the thought of new adventures in a foreign land. It seems the boy's excitement was short lived. The horrors of wintry Passchendaele put paid to that. Jack seemed reluctant to discuss this time in detail, like many men of his time who carried repressed memories they could have better lived without. What he did tell me was his and Jim's war was thankfully cut short after the shrapnel from a bomb exploded near them in no man's land rendering them both incapable of further combat.

After being dispatched to the nearest field hospital, it turned out Jim's injuries were the more severe and part of his right leg needing to be amputated. Jack's shattered knee joint meant his war was over too. Jack explained this was a time he and his mucker would have to dig deep to see any joy in their future crippled lives.

Jack, becoming very emotional, explained the following couple of years cemented his and Jim's already strong friendship. Prosthetics at this time was in its infancy and Jim was fitted with a crude but effective lower leg attachment whilst Jack needed a stirrup like attachment to act as a brace to restrict movement. In a world that demanded you earn your keep, this would be a testing time for our heroes. Jack explained the wisdom in the saying of 'necessity being the mother of invention'. Both settled back into the bosom of their poor but loving families. The two boys put their heads together in the hope of coming up with something, anything, that would give them hope for the future.

Jack explained this is where Lady Luck played her hand. Very soon a gathering in aid of the war effort was arranged at local hostelry, the Grants Arms and Jack and Jim were encouraged to go along. On their return from the Great War, Jim and Jack were awarded the status of local heroes by the local town folk. The reluctant pair found their newfound local fame at times a real burden. They understood local folk were proud to acknowledge their sacrifices, but both were uncomfortable in their newfound positions. The boys were just so happy to be home and settled back within the boundaries of the lovely village of Ramsbottom and because of their recent experiences, so appreciated the calm run of the mill routines they never thought they would miss.

The meeting in the Grant's turned out to be a lively event. Many ideas put forward by well-meaning people with folk who were in a position to pledging financial help and local women's groups arranging things such as the warm knitwear to be sent to the front etcetera.

During the course of the afternoon Jack and Jim made the acquaintance of two Bury lasses who had come along after being invited by a couple of their Ramsbottom friends. Linda and Kath were trainee nurses. The two girls fell into deep conversations with the boys. Understanding the boys' reluctance to go into detail concerning their experiences of the war, they naturally turned their attentions to the boys' injuries. Obviously Linda and Kath were not to be fooled by the boys' proud approach.

Two hours later it seemed the four of them were reluctant to take leave of one another. These were not the times where young ladies could stay for any length of time in a boy's company unless related to or were well known to their family. However the girls by their later admission were so enchanted by the two boys they just didn't want to leave their company.

As it was a lovely afternoon the four of them took a stroll by the banks of the Irwell. The girls were aware of the lads' limitations so advantage was taken of a riverside bench where the four of them could continue their eager chat of all things under the sun. One of the subjects they discussed was the need for Jack and Jim to find some form of employment now they were unfit for mill work. The girls said they would give this matter some thought also.

Jack explained that over the following months many such outings were arranged. Jack reckoned both for him and his mucker Jim, these meetings with the girls were the highlight of their lives at that time. Sometimes out of tragedy something positive comes. Linda was devastated by the death of her brother Archie to TB. Archie was one of life's indestructible optimists whose sweet smile and loving approach to life was infectious to all in his vicinity.

The passing of such wonderful folk cuts deeper than most. This and other such events fetched the four of them even closer. Their engagements were of no surprise to anyone who knew them. Linda and Jack later got into a serious chat concerning the smallholding located in the Pimhole area of Bury owned by Archie. The plot consisted of some livestock, assorted chickens, ducks, geese and half a dozen Gloucester pigs but the larger area was given over to cultivating fruit and vegetables.

The thought of the plot being taken over by a stranger was unthinkable to Linda. She put the idea to Jack, for him and Jim to take over the running of the plot between them. Jack couldn't hide his joy at the thought of himself and his best mucker working the land together. The look on his face left Linda with no need for a verbal answer. Later that day Jack put Jim in the picture concerning Linda's plan. The icing on the cake was that Archie had supplied a couple of stalls on Bury's old outside market with eggs, vegetables, occasionally fowl and sometimes even a pig. Jim, obviously in high spirits with this information, quickly suggested erecting some bee hives. "Honey is the food of the gods" smiled Jim. "Listen Jim this little enterprise is not going to make our fortune. But if we go about it right, we will make enough to keep body and soul together. It won't be easy with only two good legs between us". With a big smile gracing his face, Jack went on. "In respect to Archie we will make it work". Jim answered, also smiling "We will".

The following year was fruitful in many ways. The two couples were joined in wedlock and Jack and Jim's herculean efforts on their plot of land paid off handsomely gaining two more customers for their produce. Jim's collection of a dozen beehives at first seemed extravagant to Jack but he had to concede they were making good money from the honey. Jack reckoned he was one of the luckiest men to walk this earth. Firstly he had married his very own soul mate and secondly his working days were to be spent in the company of his best mucker, working the land and rearing livestock, which they both so enjoyed.

Jack looked me in the eye and said, "Eamon, my life has been filled with joy and contentment." Now because most of the people he loved had passed on, death held no fear for him. Occasionally Jack would meet up with Jim's widow Kath. Sadly Kath's worsening dementia meant their meetings tended to be more sad than enjoyable.

As tired as I was, I was so wrapped up in Jack's life story I was shocked when I glanced at my watch, which revealed the time to be 1.30 am.

"Well Jack, its 1.30 in the morning and we had better get ourselves some sleep".

"I'm sorry son for going on with myself".

"Give over Jack, I have enjoyed myself".

With our right hands clenched and my left hand on his right shoulder, I bid my friend goodnight. As I made my way to the door,

I was stopped in my tracks by Jack saying, "Me and Jim had one great regret, it was the fact neither of us managed to father a child. I would like you to know lad, if we had, we would have been proud for them to have turned out the same as yourself".

His words affected me deeply and, unsure how to react, I mumbled, "Thanks Jack".

As you can guess I spent a restless night going over the day's events. Within a couple of years, I would be married and move away to Radcliffe. I was made aware of Jack's passing by a notice in the Bury Times. I turned up at St Marie's Church on Manchester Road for the funeral mass to join just half a dozen folk paying their respects. I don't think I appreciated it at the time, but I realise now Jack had a massive effect on the man I would become.

It felt so wrong that this lovely fella, a good Christian man, on his way to his resting place had just a handful of folk to witness his passing. Perhaps that is the way it sometimes is, even with great people like Jack who had lived to an age where he had witnessed the demise of most of his family and friends. What a sad thought!

As the carefree days of our youth melt away into the ether we tend to spend more time in reflection. Speaking personally I tend to spend more time than I probably should in this way. No one escapes the times of their lives where we are regularly confronted by life's dilemmas; if there was a league for these situations, I would almost definitely have been in the promotion zone.

I have finally come to the realisation that if you live in the hope your life is going to run like a Mills and Boon novel, well, you are setting yourself up for many falls. I can honestly say I have done my damnedest to keep all the folks I am involved with, family and friends etcetera hunky dory. It seems no matter how hard I tried, I always still managed to upset someone.

So after many confusing decades, finally I realise my hopes were never realistic. So, better late than never, I live my life incorporating the Christian approach. Along with the realisation that there are some things I have no control over, I now accept my shortcomings and, most importantly, I stress over the serious stuff only. We all in the end must come to a situation where we can live our lives in a sustainable way. My problem was I attempted to live in a way that I thought would please others. Basically I desperately wanted to be popular, and if that meant not being true to myself, then so be it. Anyone reading this will see this as a silly or even dangerous approach to life. Having finally released myself from the shackles of self-delusion, I cannot tell you good it feels to just be myself (warts and all).

27.

RELATIONSHIPS

Looking back at the problematic situations I periodically created for folk I was supposed to love made it obvious I had, using a modern term, 'issues'. Whilst prancing through life enjoying remarks about what a grand lad I was the truth was, when push came to shove, I was a selfish bastard! Sorry, it's true. It is really strange to me now to look back and be painfully honest with myself. At one time I would, like many others, look for excuses for my actions, confessing to mates about some of the rotten capers I had got up to.

"Cor blimey Eamon, you are just one of the lads, no different".

Trouble was I knew different. Some of the stunts I pulled were nothing short of evil. This sounds pretty grim.

The good news is that redemption is on offer to everyone. The crazy thing is I was a kid who believed in happy endings. We were fetched up on them. The best programmes and films all ended well: Bonanza, Little House on the Prairie, Brief Encounter, the Incredible Journey, Kung Fu. I believed in the classic Love Story. I came from a loving family of grafters. In my head I had it all planned. As soon as I felt that special feeling with some lass, we would get married, have a houseful of kids. I would work my fingers to the bone, and live happily ever after. I was brought up a Christian and this is what good Christians do. I entered my two previous marriages with that determined conviction. Both girls gave all they had, even when my cruel unfaithful ways left them nothing to hang on to. I had them feeling so worthless; they both became easy prey for any bloke who showed them any affection. Who could blame them? Certainly not me.

The results of my actions nearly destroyed me. Two lovely girls I never deserved put into situations they would never have chosen. I, myself, sinking into a mental quagmire of my own making. These were the times I just existed. I was not living. Oh, I made the appropriate noises, answering folk's questions. I managed to quell the concerns of worried family members and work colleagues with performances Olivier would have been proud of. Drink and fags were my escape from these all these constant pressures.

It seems at stressful times most of us turn to any crutch that brings even the smallest, briefest relief, even if that crutch is mental oblivion. You would think after all this I would have learned my lesson. Not me. I was lucky enough to meet a gorgeous, funny and intelligent girl. From the start I knew there was something special about Sue. What a darlin'. A divorcee and good mother to two bonny lads and a lovely girl. A big fine house for them all to live in.

To be fair things went so well, I kept thinking this couldn't last. But it did. Two years on and things were still grand. Around this time, Sue very tactfully hinted how many folk had commented what a well-suited couple we made but it went straight over my head. Our arrangement of certain days at mine, other days at Sue's and out together on Saturdays, usually ending up at the White Lion, suited me just fine. Why fix a ticking clock.

Well selfish old me just carried on tickety boo. Delicate hints ignored I sailed on with the wind at my back. Another year and a half passed and my happy sailing was brought to a standstill by a storm that would send me to the bottom of the ocean.

One Sunday night Sue said she would be calling to mine for a chat. I could tell by her voice, something was wrong. Well it couldn't be anything too serious. We had not had a row. Sue had seemed a little distant for a week or so but that was about it. So I prepared well. Nice bottle of wine, a supermarket carry out for two, atmosphere, lighting all set. I answered the expected knock. "Hi darlin". A hug, followed by me passing Sue her glass of red wine. After clinking glasses, I said, "so what do we need to chat about?"

"Eamon, I really do love you". These words filled me with nervous fear. "I never doubted it darlin'".

There then followed an uncomfortable silence, during which I searched Sue's face for some sign she wasn't going to say what I was dreading.

Alas, although she stumbled and at times needed to catch her breath, in a low unsteady voice Sue finally broke the news that would break my heart. She had met some fella who she really liked and didn't want to do anything underhand. As we both sat on my sofa, tears streaming down both our faces, holding hands, in desperation I said, "why don't we get married?" At first I sensed Sue revealed some interest.

"It's too late Eamon. Three and a half years we have been together, with no sign of even an engagement. No, I hate seeing you so hurt, but I have made my mind up".

To her credit Sue sat up all night listening to my emotional pleading. At one point I asked Sue to listen to some really hard-hitting country songs. What I was hoping for God only knows. Maybe hoping the heart-breaking lyrics would sway her mind.

With one track I thought I had struck gold. That track was Garth Brooks *The Dance*. After listening to the track Sue broke down saying, "I might be making a big mistake".

For some reason, probably finally realising what I was doing was wrong, I said, "No you're not Sue. You must keep to your decision and if it doesn't work out, well I will be waiting for you". By the time we had talked ourselves to a standstill, dawn was breaking. Sue's Mum had charge of the kids but as she was due in work early, Sue left my home around 7 am. I waited at the 471 bus stop with her. As her bus approached we shared a last hug. You can imagine how the next couple of weeks were spent.

28.

A NEW START

I promise you now, for any reader still in attendance, no more romantic trials. Hopefully I can keep your interest with other subjects. So here we are 2010 and I am married to Dawn, who along with her lovely daughter Tanya and son Shane and their partners are grand folk that have a really calming effect on me. Another big plus are two more lovely grandkids to go with my eldest son's four, each real characters in their own right.

My eldest son Lee is a cracking lad who loves his job as a plasterer and usually arrives back home shattered but content in himself. Megan, my daughter reminds me so much of a classic Irish Colleen. Gorgeous. Ethan, my youngest is a big handsome comic who sees his future as a soldier. This has me a little worried but, as he says, "Dad, there is nothing here for me." My days now I enjoy so much. As anyone who has their own house knows, there is plenty to keep a fella busy seven days a week if they have a mind.

On market days I head down to my Brother John's place on Killon Street. Arthritis has severely compromised John's mobility. After calling on John followed by a bit of shopping I then head for Costa Coffee in Bury's market square, where I meet up at 1 pm with my retired mates who make up the Brew Gang.

I have known Paul for many years. Formerly Tottington United footy manager and known for a couple of sightings performing heroics in his role of British Gas man extraordinaire. In later years I was relocated to the round named Elton Fold. As Paul lived at this time on Holcombe Avenue, which was on my new round, our paths would cross occasionally. Mostly it would be Paul's son, Scott who I would pass on their garden path.

One day as I was approaching Scott on the street, expecting just the usual, "all reet cocker?"

"Yeah, you?"

"Sound".

This day Scott replied, "Not really".

"What's up cocker?"

"My Dad, he has got cancer of the oesophagus".

"Oh, God Scott I am so sorry. You know they can work wonders now if they catch it early. Listen, don't know about you, but I am gonna say a little prayer for him".

Scott didn't look too impressed, which to be honest I half expected.

"What's to lose?"

The following months must have been really tough for Paul. Each time I passed the window to deliver their mail, Paul lay on the couch and some days he hadn't the strength to answer my wave. Poor lad. I confess I feared the worst. As the months passed a pattern of highs and lows became the norm. What a vicious disease cancer is. Thankfully Paul was in no mood to roll over. Oh no! In good health, Paul was a powerful man. That physical strength combined with the just as important inner strength gave Paul the edge. It would be a long hard battle. But he did it. From then on each day Paul would slowly regain his strength. Cannot tell you how made up I was when informed of this. For one reason or another I saw little of Paul. Cannot say at this time Paul and me were close. He was just a fella I sensed was a decent bloke.

Fast forward once again to early 2012. I am sat outside Costa Coffee watching the rest of the world going about their business. I had been there about twenty minutes when Paul approached where I was sat.

"Look who it is, how the devil are ya?"

"I'm okay, how are you?" Paul replied,

"I'm grand, not seen you in ages". Paul sat down beside me.

I said, "hang on I will get you a brew".

This was the beginning of a friendship that I valued on a par with family members. Paul informed me the gas board had retired him on ill health grounds several years before. This news fetched an involuntary smile to my face. All I could think was, another free man, time on his hands, and as most of our friends were wage slaves, it would be grand to have a mucker who enjoyed the same things as myself. Time would tell.

I was shocked when Paul told me him and his wife had parted company. "Sorry to hear that cocker".

"It's okay, we are still friends which is good. We had some grand holidays after I recovered".

Paul talked so passionately about South Africa, it felt like I had been there myself. He loved the place.

Paul and his wife had an apartment in Tenerife. This apartment would serve as Paul's bolthole for up to five weeks a year. Within weeks Paul and me were spending a lot of time together. My wife, Dawn, thought Paul was brilliant. Dawn's run in with the big C has had lasting effects on her quality of life. Being a home bird has helped in this respect.

It was not long before Paul and me found ourselves in a routine that suited us both. Tuesday would find us setting out on walking expeditions that would take us to Edgeworth, the three reservoirs – Jumbles, Entwistle, Waho – Burrs Country Park, down Gigg, Bury and Bolton Canal and Birtle. The latter supplied us with a bit of a surprise.

One day I coaxed Paul into leaving our well-trodden path and making an excursion into the unknown. So we took a left along a narrow path, hedged on the right with evergreens, on the left an array of deciduous trees and bushes that ran down to a large pond. Paul and me both thought the same, whoever owns the large house that overlooked this huge pond and garden was not short of funds and were so lucky to wake up to this view every morning.

The surprise waiting for the two of us was located at the end of this path. At the end of the path we found ourselves stood at the top of a stone staircase that descended underneath a fine stone built house. Yes, incredibly our right of way took us beneath this house. Chuckling we made our way along the passageway that fetched us out into a sort of courtyard. From here we took a right by the same big old terraced homes. We were then back on the track that would take us by the Old Birtle School house then over by the golf course and on up to Dunham Farm, which leads to a view over Ashworth Valley that takes your breath away. Gone on a bit there, sorry!

Wednesdays and Fridays our arrangements were identical. At 1pm you would find us at Costa Coffee. Before we met Paul religiously called at Chadwick's stall for two black puddings. He's obviously feeling better. So 1pm saw Paul and me sat side-by-side chatting away. Being social creatures and no longer in the flush of youth, it seemed there was a steady stream of old muckers and acquaintances stopping for a catch up.

Paul and me always enjoyed these diversions. The majority of these folk tended to belong to the mature generation. The reason was simply that the younger folk would be working at the time we were there. The two of us felt blessed. We realised it was serious health issues that allowed us our privileged lifestyle. We had both completed forty years of unbroken toil before our working lives were brought to an end. We felt lucky but not embarrassed.

One of the reasons we chose Costa was the two shop managers, Nicola and Sean. Loveable lunatics that never hid their obvious enjoyment of their work. It was impossible not to get caught up in their joyful characters. To my delight there were many occasions when folk would roll up with a copy of my book for me to sign. Paul would come out with comments like, "I told you someone would buy one Eamon. Now, don't forget, when you have coloured it all in, fetch it back and he will give you a free one."

"Very droll Mr Leach!"

Come 2.30pm the two of us set off for the inside market to 'Big Jim's Café'. Here we would meet up with other regular 'Brew Gang' members. Tony Filbin, Mick O'Reilly, Tom Briggs, Dave Woods and a married couple, Ian and Muriel. Folk who stopped for a chat on a regular basis were local footy hero George Jones, John Wolfendon and the only fella who could out talk any of us, Wally Kane. This amiable Scotsman has such skill in relaying his stories he could captivate a wooden post. Wally came down from his native Scotland to join the worthy cause of Bury FC's push for honours in the early 70s. He was in good company with lads the calibre of Brian Green, Nello, Dave Wolfendon. Unbelievably none of these talented lads made the grade. Bury FC must have been one hell of a team to have kept these lads out.

Paul and me really enjoyed our cafe days. We never spent too long without visits from an array of characters that added colour to our day and we just never knew what to expect. It was always that bit more special when someone neither of us had seen for years turned up. Surprisingly this happened pretty regularly. It seems we all enjoy catching up with old friends. Boy, girl, old, young, it mattered not.

Our Saturdays were just as regimented. Paul would pick me up at mine around 10am. We would then set off for a chosen local walking area. On one occasion we found ourselves within the borders of the picturesque and historically rich Irwell Vale. Being a real fan of local history, this was a real find. Upon arriving at Chatterton we came across a large field. A notice board informed us of a riot by mill workers in 1828. It seemed that, as in many other areas of this land, mill workers were becoming incensed due to the technological advances that the industrial revolution brought. You can imagine! You and your workmates are called together one day to be informed that due to the new spinning and weaving machines only half of you were now needed. Don't know about you, but I wouldn't have been happy. These were the days where very few folk sought work outside their own town or village and this would have been a massive blow. Thinking about it, I'm not sure how I would of reacted. Who can say until you are in that position? Sadly the lads and girls who worked at Aitkens Mill chose to riot. The mill owner, Thomas Aitken, called in the government troops. Unbelievably the troops adopted a shoot to kill stand. Four men and one woman were killed. I would not liked to have been Mr Aitken after this. Speaking personally, I could never have come to terms with my actions. Knowing nearly every villager hated you with a passion, but because of the simple facts of life, they had to seek employment with you.

Paul's interest in local history was slight at best. It tickled me as the months passed, he would come rushing up to me, telling me I must come with him as he had found a cottage, house, whatever that he was sure was eighteenth century.

"You can tell Eam, it's got those brick window frames. Come on you have gotta see this".

"You seem very excited Paul for someone who not so long ago thought all this was boring".

"Well you have brainwashed me. Ha! Ha".

Harry, my Jack Russell come Staffordshire terrier, always accompanied us on our travels. Paul reckoned I had brainwashed poor Harry as well. Reckoned he found Harry sat outside an ancient cottage, straining to make out the faded date stone. I always felt happier when there was a date stone on a building we discovered. Sometimes, not often, we were accompanied on our treks by our Michael, Martin Farnworth or our Scottish mucker Kenny Buckle.

On these occasions we would invariably call in at one of the many grand old public houses we would pass on our way. The Pack Horse at Birtle, the Shoulder of Mutton at Holcombe or the White Horse at Edgworth. It was at this time that members of my family decided I was basing my life on the protagonists of *Last of the Summer Wine*. I, of course was Compo!

On one of our many excursions to Edgeworth we came across the burial place of one Richard Barlow. Richard's grave was enclosed by a low stone wall around 15 feet square. The original grave stone was laid flat and time and the weather had left the inscription unreadable, As the original engraving was pretty worn and in places broken, a generous benefactor had paid for a new stone. The story goes Richard was the local preacher who spent his time spreading the gospel to the sparse local folk. As part of his covenant Richard was never to marry or have children. Well, this strong-minded fella decided he wanted both and, because of this, when Richard died he was not allowed to be laid down in consecrated land. Obviously there must have been enough of his flock who thankfully still loved the man. His resting place, because of a bench, placed along the entrance wall, became one of Paul's and myself's favourite places to sit and ponder. The view it offered us as we ate our lunch was breath-taking.

After completing our walk, Paul would drop me home. He would then return home to change and get a bit to eat and I would do the same. We would meet up again, along with several of our muckers, before the 2pm kick off at Elton Vale to watch either the first or second team giving their all for the entertainment of the usually decent crowd. At first team games John Nuttall, who works hard for the Vale, organised everything from matches to collecting subs (incredibly our lads paid £3 subs, the same I paid donkey's years before). Included in this was pie and peas, not bad eh? He would come round during the game selling match programmes for £1 that include a raffle ticket that gave you the chance to win a bottle of wine. We know the players really appreciated our presence, as we would stand to one side of the goal and on the occasions we scored, well let's say we were very vocal and they loved it. It gave them a lift.

After the game we would head for the comfort of the Elton Vale Clubhouse where the lads would enjoy a couple of pints. Not being a drinker, Margaret and Shirley kept me happy with mugs of good strong tea. The game we had just watched would be dissected and we would commiserate or celebrate with managers Bill Mundy and Phil Hartley. The time would too quickly come round where we would bid our farewells to the assembled folk. The lads I was with would need to get home to shower and change, then hit the pubs around Bury town centre. The only pub they would never pass was the White Lion on Bolton Street. Other pubs had in theory more going for them. In reality the Lion was always heaving with folk who found its relaxed friendly atmosphere suited them down to the ground. Not being a drinker now, my nights out were fewer than days gone by. This was not by choice. After my heart attack in 2003, 2010 saw me contract diabetes. On the occasions I partook of the black stuff, I paid dearly for my enjoyment. To the point I made the decision to end my love affair with Mr Guinness' wonderful brew.

So nowadays when embarking on a night out, soda water and a slice of lemon is my tipple of choice. All right for several drinks, but when you end up having around 10, well, then comes the time when all around you are cracking up over some – to you in your sober state – unfunny comment. Then you realise if you had had the same amount of alcohol, you would be laughing with them. Up to the time my drinking partners lose the power to converse coherently I would really enjoy their company. After, well, I sought less intoxicated company.

29.

WAYNE PAYS A VISIT

"Hi Wayne, how's it going?"

"Not bad Eamon, passing your place Sunday afternoon".

"Magic, call in we will have a brew and a chat".

This phone conversation was the result of a chance meeting with Wayne up Bury the week before. I always admired Wayne for, as a lad from farming stock, he had certainly made the most of his ability to find the back of the net with a football. Also the date stone over his farmhouse door from 1710 was the oldest me and my mucker Leachy ever found within Burys' borders. There are certainly older buildings around, but these do not show date stones, of which, as you have guessed, I am very fond. Can you imagine what our fair town would have looked like in the year 1710? Wouldn't it be grand just to be transported back to then? Just a spirit free to roam around, hoping to see sights you may recognise. Bury would be almost unrecognisable from the present day. Listening in on conversations, hoping to find in their talk an insight into the lives they led.

As horses were kings of the road, the thought of being a Lancashire cowboy would have so appealed to me. With my luck, I would have been a child miner; trapped in permanent darkness, where the sun never shines, in one of the many mines hereabouts. Life for most folk would have been tough back then. Looking back, has it ever been any different? Sorry! I keep drifting.

Sunday afternoon came round, a knock on the door. Wayne stood there with his trusty bike.

"Go round the back Wayne, your bike will be safer. I'll put the kettle on".

Our chairs placed so Wayne and me were facing one another. Now up to this point, apart from going through the accepted pleasantries I had never had a conversation with Wayne. So here goes.

"Tea or coffee Wayne?"

"Tea please. Would you let the water go off the boil for mine. Leave the tea bag in. Just a touch of milk."

He then insisted I return the milk immediately back to the fridge.

"Right, okay Wayne". I realised I was in the company of a farmer's lad. A breed of their own, so little quirks like this hardly come under the heading of major upset.

Wayne and me were sat in my kitchen for around three hours. With Wayne doing most of the talking, by the time he began donning his biking gear, I felt like I knew this man pretty well. Early on Wayne informed me he was working on laying the metro line, near Manchester airport. This came as news to me. I assumed he was still delivering cold meats to local butchers. It turned out Wayne cycled most of the way to his work from the farm on Woodhill Road and then at the end of his working day cycled back. These almost super human energy levels are obviously what carried him to heights, which the likes of myself could only dream. It seems his driving force came from his old fella Jim.

Jim, no mean player himself, made the Bury boys side where he was assured he would become a Bury FC player while still in his teens. For one reason or another, this never came to fruition and resulted in Jim deciding early on that his son would fulfil his lost prophecy. Jim adopted the old school trait. The trait that believed that if you wanted to achieve anything, then it must be done through hard work. The result of this was that young Wayne followed in his Dad's footsteps in making the Bury Boys Team. Up to an hour before their matches, Jim would have his son working like a donkey. How the poor lad had the energy to charge about a field for ninety minutes is solely down to his unbelievable energy levels.

His dad instilled in young Wayne a steely determination to 'make the grade'. If he failed, waiting for him was a life of toil on his father's farm and that was the last thing young Wayne wanted. Then, to his credit, he forced his way into the Bury team and cultivated a good relationship with his manager, Bobby Smith. In return, Smith would mould this young man of the soil into an accomplished centre-forward whose sheer stamina together with an instinct to find the net, set him apart at this time.

It was not long before sleeping giants Sunderland came knocking. How good is that? What a dream playing for the Roker fans, fans who will cheer you to the ends of the earth. Wayne waxed lyrical about the legendary 'Roker roar', which he found inspiring. Against Bristol Rovers in his second season Wayne scored a hat trick. Can you imagine it! As lads who did not quite make it, and there are a good few in Bury, we certainly can imagine. In truth these thoughts pass through most lads' minds.

Wayne is without doubt a very humble sort of fella, a trait I find so attractive. Wayne informed me he considered his team mates from Bury boys days such as John Oliviero, Ian Meadowcroft, Dave Powell and Gary Wilcox were all, skill wise, better players than himself. On this occasion I reckon Wayne was maybe a little too humble.

Wayne then moved on to Leeds United, who also could be described as sleeping giants, and played with the likes of Eddie Grey, Paul Madeley and Trevor Cherry. It must have been so humbling for Wayne. Then again, let's not forget he was there on merit. This lad from a compromised start, by sheer determination and hard work, reached a level where he was sharing the pitch with team-mates who had reached legendary status. He certainly had my respect. Also he is a smashing chap to boot. "Well done Wayne".

The only time we went off the subject of footy was when I asked Wayne to tell me a little of the history of Entwistle Farm. Wayne had little knowledge of its origins, only living memory. Wayne's uncle Eric was terrified one day by the sight of a band of German and Italian soldiers marching down Woodhill Road. As this was during wartime it certainly gave them a shock. These lads would have been POW's who were inmates from the bleach works at Burrs.

There is also a moving story concerning Wayne's Gran and sister. In 1937 while out on the milk round, they arrived at one of their regular houses in Irwell Street. After receiving no answer, they entered the property. They were to find a baby under a bed. This child, Jim Bell, was taken back to the farm. The child's father explained he could not look after the child and did not know anyone else who could. Apparently this man's wife had passed on. In true Christian spirit Jim the baby would be reared by Wayne's Great Grandma Ellen. We owe this information to Wayne's Auntie Molly Smith of Walmersley to whom I gave my thanks.

Wayne scoring his last goal for Sunderland before his move to Leeds.

30.

SECOND VISIT

A few weeks later I paid Wayne a visit at the very old farmhouse on Woodhill Road. The thought of entering a building that was completed in 1710 excited me no end and so one Sunday afternoon I set out on my trusty old bike from my home in Breightmet, having to stay alert to negotiate the many potholes that grace the bicycle lanes on the A58. As I neared Bury Bridge, the half expected rain came down, accompanied by a very strong headwind that ensured the rest of my journey seemed a whole lot further.

Finally arriving at the farmhouse, my nostrils were greeted by a very powerful odour you would only find in the farmyards of our green and pleasant land. After parking my bike up I gave the farm door a good knock. Receiving no answer, I decided to give Wayne a ring on his mobile. I knew on most Sundays Wayne took local blind folk on long bicycle rides. He informed me the reason he was not home at our agreed time of 3pm was that one of the other bikes had suffered a puncture. It would be after 3.30 pm he expected to arrive home.

"Okay Wayne, see you later".

Well, over half an hour to kill, I crouched into the doorway in a vain effort to keep out of the rain. Fifteen long minutes dragged by, my only entertainment provided by a cow inside the cowshed who periodically stuck his or her head through a hole in the shed wall that seemed to have been cut out so this beast could, like a giant cuckoo clock, stick its head through the hole and moo to its hearts content. Then a chap appeared from the rear of the farmhouse.

"Allreet," he said.

"Yeah, waiting on Wayne".

"Right you are". He then carried on his way. As I said, farmers tend to have more quirks than the rest of us.

Another five minutes dragged past, then a bonny young lass came up to me.

"Hiya, what are you doing?"

"Waiting on Wayne."

"Don't stand in the rain, come on, follow me". She led me round the back, showed me where to park my bike, and led through what I realised was the kitchen door. I was introduced to the young girl's Gran who turned out to be Wayne's Mum. We went through the usual Lancashire greeting. I then sat myself down at a large dining table. After a short chat during which Wayne's Mum gave me the impression there was not much communication between herself and her son, she left me for a while. During this time I took in all I could of this ancient kitchen which was now graced with modern units and appliances. A little saddened by this, I hoped Wayne would maybe show me another part of the house.

Think I am turning into a bit of an anorak where old buildings are concerned. Even though this kitchen sported a modern style, over three hundred years of families have passed through these walls. Bet they could tell some tales. My thoughtful reverie was brought to an end by the arrival of the man himself. Wayne's appearance seemed intact enough. He had informed me the week before he had come off his bike on Bolton Road near the zebra crossing at Colville Drive and needed thirty stiches for the wounds he received.

"Allreet cocker?"

"Yeah, you?"

"Fine." Wayne then set about making a brew and cutting a slice of cheesecake each. I had to inform Wayne I would not be able to partake of the cheesecake as I had already that day had my weekly treat of a bowl of sticky toffee pudding and my diabetes would allow no more. It was comical watching and listening to Wayne having a conversation with himself. Told off many times for doing the same, I could hardly criticise.

As I needed to confirm a few facts concerning Wayne's story, he suggested we move to a room he told me they rarely used. Magic, could hardly wait. I was not disappointed. It felt like we had boarded the 'Marie Celeste'. The room retained its original decoration. Also you could sense this room had received a woman's touch. The walls and the ceiling were adorned with chandelier-type high fittings. To my delight the room was crammed with antique ornaments and photographs.

Wayne carried on chatting as I inspected the things that took my interest. Then on a small shelf near the high dado rail I spotted an orange football. Wayne caught my gaze.

"That's the ball with which I scored a hat trick for Sunderland Eamon".

Wayne's voice became very vague as I stared at the forlorn look-ing football. A lovely reminder of past glories! After making sure I had what I needed, I took Wayne's hand in a heartfelt handshake. I won't become a stranger to Wayne, I really like the man and to me his sometimes eccentric ways make him more endearing. Plus any chance I got to see more of the farmhouse I would take it.

31.

DAMP IN BRANGY

"Where to today, Mr Leach?"

"Thought we would try round Kirklees for a change."

"Sounds good."

Paul's black Ford Focus was a regular visitor outside my Breightmet home, boot open, ready for me to deposit my rucksack. I would then settle into the passenger seat with my dog Harry between my legs. Harry always accompanied Paul and me on our twice-weekly walks. I had to be very careful not to mention Paul's name before his arrival, or jangle his lead, as he simply got too excited.

Paul turned the car round and headed for Bury. We parked up just off Brangy Road near the shops. Paul led the way. He informed me we would be passing through by Tower Farm, Greenmount, but would end up in Brangy.

"Right you are".

So off we set. This being our Tuesday walk, it would be more relaxed than the Saturday walk. There tended to be at least four of us on Saturday mornings. Tuesday was always just Paul and me, which gave me a chance to quiz him about his weekend.

The week before we had had a row when Paul told me after his usual night out round Bury Centre he had opted to drive his car instead of taking a taxi home.

"You are joking," I went on one, really ripped strips off him. "Tell you what Paul, do that again, we are done".

"Calm down, bloody hell Eam. Keep your hair on".

"Paul this is serious".

"I drove really carefully," he said. I just stared at him.

"Okay, okay I promise never to do it again".

"Right, we will say no more".

I knew he was sincere, which made me feel instantly calmer. So I asked, "who was out on Saturday night round town?"

"Your Michael was out".

"Right, was he on good form?"

"Yeah, we had last orders in the White Lion. It was heaving. Good artist on".

"Don't tell me you got up?"

"Nagh, but your kid did".

"You are joking! He must have had a few".

"Your kid's all right until he starts on the bloody whisky".

"I know, he loves the bloody stuff. Thing is it seems to enliven him. Always knocks me for six. Who else was out?"

"Seen Eric Greenhalgh with Pete Lee in Molloys, Al Jones and Al Keown in the Robert Peel. Strangely, by the time your kid and me reached the Two Tubs, we couldn't recognise anyone, even ourselves".

Our conversation was stopped by the comical sight of Harry getting fruity with a greyhound. Harry is a Jack Russell, Staff cross and stands about nine inches at the shoulder. You can imagine. Apologising as I am pulling Harry away, the owner of the greyhound, a John Thorpe lookalike, said, "no problem, my dog's a he".

In unison the three of us turned our heads in Harry's direction. The chap then said, "looks like you have a fine gay dog".

"Thank you very much". On we went, with me giving Harry a sideways curious look.

Just after the bird sanctuary at Kirklees we found ourselves trudging through a swampy field. On our left were the back gardens of Birks Drive, on our right a barbed wire fence. Obviously we should not have been walking on this land.

"Mr Leach, you have turned us into trespassers. Cannot understand it, well, come on let's get a wiggle on".

So we headed to an area where the barbed wire fence joined up with a small brick building around five foot high and twelve feet long. A slow running stream around eight feet across ran right up to the bricks and, rather than attempt climbing the wire fence, we decided to creep along a thin ledge running the length of the brick building. Paul went first, revealing the dexterity of a primate, using his hands to cling to the single brick surround of the build. So Paul stood on Garside Hey Road with Harry at this side waiting for me to join them. You just know don't you? It seems some things seem inevitable.

Well I am creeping along just fine, then about three feet from home, the brick I am clinging to, came away in my hand. Apparently I screamed like a girl. Worryingly, I sank slowly down into the sludge up to my chest.

"Paul, for God's sake get a stick or something. Come on hurry up!"

It was no use, the bugger could not get up off the floor. Then Harry jumped in, swimming round me barking his head off. By this time I was gripped by a genuine fear Paul was going to be too late by the time he got himself together to help me out.

"Paul pull yourself together, you bloody idiot".

Still laughing and with tears streaming down his face, he made his way to the bank. Then, using the towel we use for drying Harry, he flung one end out to me. Gripping the towel for all I was worth, Paul very slowly pulled me over to him. Must have been five minutes in all. Just seemed longer. As I hauled myself onto the bank, accompanied by a dull sucking noise, Paul lost it again. Looking down at myself, dripping black sludge from my chest down, I joined in the laughing. What a sight!

As we made our way up Garside Hey Road, every step I took

produced a loud squelch. I reckon we did not stop laughing until we reached Brangy Road. Even Harry had a smile as we made our way to Paul's car.

"Well Mr Leach I cannot get in the car like this".

Nothing else for it, off came the lot, apart from my soaking trollies. The offending gear was shoved into a plastic bag and we were off.

"Now listen Mr Leach. Don't bloody dare have a bump or speed. Don't think I would live it down if a copper pulled us with me like this. And we cracked up again.

32.

ROUTINES

Mr Leach and me enjoyed the routines we established early on in our friendship. On the days we were not walking, each morning Mr Leach would make his way to the 'Stables', the gym attached to the Bolholt Hotel on Walshaw Road. Here he met up with several female friends, one of which Mr Leach considered to be the perfect woman. The lady in question was spoken for and made it clear anything more than friendship was off the menu.

I remember saying to Mr Leach, "well cocker, at least she has been straight with you".

"You are right Eamon, just does not make me feel any better".

It was not lost on me that Paul felt pretty lonesome at times. I found it so frustrating not to be able to help my best mate in this matter.

Like many blokes, Paul sought comfort in a bottle. I always thought at these times that he hit the drink a little hard and I relied on mutual friends for updates. After becoming diabetic I rarely went out at weekends. Mainly reunions and birthdays. The exception being the occasions Paul and me, at the end of certain walks, found ourselves stood outside a pub that was so inviting it was beyond either of us to walk on. The Strawberry Duck and the Pack Horse at Birtle are perfect examples. To be fair I have only seen Paul paralytic while enjoying a holiday in Tenerife. Me and my wife Dawn joined Paul at his lovely apartment there in Los Gigantes. At this time one of Paul's muckers Mark Vernon and his gorgeous wife Elena, who happened to be with child, were also present. It's fair to say most folk go a bit daft with the drink while on holiday. Well this night, while Dawn and me decided on a quiet night in, Paul and Mark attired in their glad rags, set off for their night on the town. Dawn and me settled ourselves with all we could wish for on the raised balcony overlooking this lovely little town. The more we relaxed it seemed the town relaxed in unison.

As darkness fell it just added to an already relaxed mood. There is something hypnotic about staring out to sea against a backdrop of a spectacularly lit sky. God, I feel like bursting into poetry! Anyway, as time passed the couple of glasses of red wine me and Dawn had shared left the two of us feeling happily drowsy. It must have been around 1.30am when we retired to the comfort of our bed. At around 3.30am came a loud bang on the apartment door. Upon answering it, we were greeted by a not too sober Mr Vernon holding up an even less sober Mr Leach.

"Okay Mark, we will take over from here".

It must have taken me a good half hour to finally get Mr Leach tucked up in bed whilst having to listen to drunken renditions of, strangely *Flower of Scotland*. Suddenly he became quiet, looked me straight in the eyes and said, "Seriously Eam, I think Mark has a drink problem".

"Right you are Mr Leach. Now you be a good boy, get a good night's sleep and I will fetch you a nice brew in the morning and, if you are really good, a slice of toast". I closed the bedroom door as Paul began another verse of *Flower of Scotland*.

The next morning Paul looked and said he felt grand. I must admit, Paul's tolerance of alcohol worried me. For the rest of the holiday Paul remained on great form. He always took the time and trouble to make sure me and Dawn had a ball. I loved him for his thoughtfulness.

33.

BACK TO REALITY

Much as I enjoyed our holiday, it felt so good to settle back into our routine of going on brilliant walks, enjoying the company of the brew gang and watching our team Elton Vale at the weekend. Not everybody's cup of tea but Paul and me loved it. I kept thinking of any unattached lassies I knew who maybe I could accidently arrange for Paul to meet. For some reason my efforts to this end proved fruitless. Thankfully the man himself began at last to have some luck. The trouble Paul had was that each woman he met he tended to compare them, unfairly in my mind, to the lady he considered a gift to man. One of these ladies, who I considered a cracker, showed a lot of interest in Paul. Janet is the sister of my old workmate at Royal Mail, Geoff Kenyon. The Kenyon's are a family I thought of as good solid Bury folk. As a result I kept reminding Paul what a grand lass she was and probably went a bit over the top. I tried to impress on him the importance of treating her well.

Eventually, as they patronised the same pubs up town, Molloys and the brilliant White Lion, I decided to let it be. What will be will be. I know they went on a couple of picnics, which seemed very promising. While out on our walks, being the times we tended to discuss the deeper subjects in life, Paul was non-committal. I knew some of Paul's other mates were able to influence his judgement more than they should.

"Mr Leach, be your own man. You are nobody's fool. Trust your own gut feeling".

"How many times have you been married Eam"?

What could I say? Paul really missed family life. He needed the structure and intimacy it involved. He had loads of good mates. He also spent a lot of time on his lonesome.

Dez, Paul's brother-in-law, was into organising dinners and gigs with hundreds of folk attending. Dez always insisted 'our Paul' attended all these functions. To be fair, Paul usually really enjoyed the events. There came a time when our team, Elton Vale, needed an injection of funds. Paul, no mean organiser himself, set to work with real conviction, less than well assisted by our Michael, me and Mr Buckle who were meant to make up the Committee. Basically Paul was left to his own devices. The fact it went ahead at all was purely down to Paul's determination.

Around four weeks before the big night Paul and me were sat in Big Jim's cafe awaiting the arrival of the other brew members when a vivacious blonde lass of around 46 came and sat with us. Hazel she was called. She explained she was meeting up with her Mum and would we mind. Well, one thing I knew for sure was Paul certainly did not mind. God no! In short the two of them really hit it off.

By the time Hazel's Mum joined us, Paul was smitten.

"My God Mr Leach, you have only just met the girl".

"I know, I know, just really like her Eam. Is she single?"

"She's separated. Well, listen Paul don't get in too deep".

"Does she have kids"?

"Yes. Just take it slowly".

The weeks running up to the big night at the Vale Club saw Paul and Hazel seeing a lot of each other. During those short weeks Paul must have purchased half a dozen jackets from the charity shops on the Rock. I was gobsmacked by the fact each of these jackets fit Paul so well. You would swear they were made to measure.

"Don't tell me Eam, it fits me perfect".

"Paul I kid you not, I wouldn't say it if it wasn't true". This conversation preceded every purchase.

For a lad who would not be seen entering a charity shop, he was turning out to be one of their best customers. So here was Mr Leach, with a wardrobe jammed with classy jackets. A week before the big night he asked me to accompany him to Loofe's clothes shop in the Millgate. Paul informed me they were in the process of relocating and were offering two-piece suits for £99.

"Paul you have a wardrobe full of good gear. Why buy a suit?"

"Eam I am telling you now, nothing looks better than a nice suit".

After finally making his choice, Paul stepped out of the changing cubicle earnestly seeking my approval. I have to say here and now Mr Leach looked a million dollars. I have always loved clothes and stood in front of me now was one the reasons. Transformed from Mr Frumpy to a classy man about town.

"Okay Mr Leachy, you were right. You look mighty fine. Get it paid for and let's head home".

The light blue, well-tailored suit was carefully placed into a yellow Loofe's bag and we were off. I always enjoyed our trips back to mine in Paul's car. We both loved good music. Paul loved Elton John, George Michael and many Irish tracks. To me his favourite CD seemed to be *Big Country's Greatest Hits*. When it came to the tracks *Chance* and *Fields of Fire* it was impossible for either of us not to add our vocals to the brilliant vocals of Stuart Adamson. Paul informed me Stuart had in a fit of depression taken his own life. A couple of times I took along my *Meat Loaf* CD and asked Paul to play *Two out of three ain't bad*. Paul and me would sing this track the whole way through. In my humble opinion one of the most beautiful love songs every written.

The following Saturday morning, me, Paul and Kenny set out for the wilds of Birtle. My dog Harry and Kenny's red setter Maddie got along just fine. So with the two of them exploring every nook and cranny, the three of us discussed the day's coming events. Paul informed me and Kenny that one of the lead singers of the ABBA tribute band was none other than Paul's estranged wife Karen's sister.

"They had better be good Mr Leach," I said, "seeing as you are forever singing their praises".

"Oh they are good, no worries on that score," said Mr Leach.

As we reached the rim of Ashworth Valley after passing through Dunham Farm, we arrived at a wooden bench a few yards down the valley. This is a great place to take time out and affords a great view of the whole valley. The three of us settled down to a flask of hot milky coffee, a sandwich each and some rich tea biscuits. In easy silence we sat there taking in the view, enjoying our mean fare, while the two dogs sat like statues watching every mouthful we swallowed, knowing each of us in turn would chuck them scraps.

After a while I asked Paul "Will Hazel be coming tonight?"

"She will. She understands I will have to keep an eye on proceedings."

"She okay with that?"

Yeah, she's sound".

"Well we will watch the Vale then make an early exit, give us plenty of time to prepare for the big night. Come on let's make a move, remind me to get some eggs from that chap on the way down to the Pack Horse. After a quick pint at the Pack, we made our way home.

34.

THE BIG DOO

I must admit getting ready that evening I felt pretty excited about this get together Paul had arranged. I knew quite a few of our old mates would be making an appearance. I always enjoyed these catch-ups, or touching base, as our Michael would say. As me and Dawn set about making ourselves presentable, I slipped a cassette into the music centre. I know using cassettes will seem pretty old fashioned to some folk, but I love them. This cassette would be filled with songs that, for one reason or another, I love.

As the intro to *Raglan Road* began – a song that may be my favourite of all time – Dawn shouted from the bedroom, "God's sake Eamon, can we have some cheerful music for a change".

Grudgingly I sympathised with Dawn. I realised my choice of music would not be to most people's taste when preparing for a night out. This was probably the Irish in me. Strange as it may seem, playing melancholy tunes had the effect of setting me up just dandy for a night of celebration. Why this is so, I know not. If it was up to me, this would be the desired preparation. Alas one must think of others.

"Just this one side, then *will* put some Tamla on".

"Okay, go on then".

Raglan Road was still playing. Has there ever been a more beautiful song? Written as a poem by the great Irish Poet Patrick Kavanagh. I must just say this name had no influence of my love for this song.

Patrick's lovely poem was put to music and, by the gift of foresight – it would be another hero of mine *Luke Kelly* of The Dubliners fame – would create for me, one of the most fabulous combinations in music history. The haunting result invariably made the hairs on the back of my neck stand on end, resulting in all other thoughts being banished from my mind, replaced by the magical tone of Kelly's voice. Sorry, gone a bit again. Hope you get my drift. I so hope you, the reader, can relate to this situation. Not all the tracks I had taped leaned towards melancholy. God no, some were very upbeat. *Cocaine Blues*, Johnny Cash, *Maids when you're young, never wed an old man*, The Dubliners, *Same Old Song*, The Four Tops. I defy anyone to sit still while that track is on but overall I confess I love sad songs.

This reminds me of the time I spent in Knightsbridge working for Henry Hargreaves. Many weekends I patronised a couple of the local Irish pubs. Towards the end of the night there would always be a few favourites like *The Old Bog Road* and the evergreen *Fields of Athenry*. Invariably tears would be flowing free from many of the Irish eyes present. It never failed to tickle me that if you offered any of these chaps a ticket home, there would be few takers. No, as much as us Irish enjoy a little misery, the rest of our get ready time would be accompanied by the brilliant music provided by the superb Tamla Label. So Dawn and me were feeling ready to enjoy a good night with folk whose company we always enjoyed, hopefully with good music, also raising a bit of money for the club we supported.

As we climbed into the taxi supplied by Elton Taxi's, we settled into a cheerful chat with the lad driving. Always enjoy a taxi ride when the driver is a talkative soul. It seemed no time had passed at all when we pulled up into the Elton Vale car park. As we passed the windows of the club, we could see there was already a good crowd gathering. Magic.

Mr Leach was at the door to take our ticket money, "Allreet cocker".

"Yeah, looking forward to it Paul. Will I get you a pint?" I asked.

"No, Hazel has just got them in".

"Right, well you're not staying on the door all night, me and our Michael will help out".

"That's good, go and get yourselves a drink. There's space on the table next to us".

"Okay, see you in a bit".

While Dawn got herself settled, I made my way to the bar.

"A bottle of your finest red please Steph".

Behind the bar that night were Steph Shaw, John McDermott, Les Duddley and John Nuttall, all good lads. Making my way back across the dance floor Sacko, Kenny Buckle and Daz Smith and their wives were taking their seats alongside Dawn and me.

"Allreet kids."

"Sound, nice of you to get the wine in Eam".

"Sorry lads, this bottle will probably last me and Dawn all night".

"Tight bugger".

"Not tight, it's just that neither of us is used to drink anymore".

"It was a joke Eam".

As there was a bit of a lull before the music started proper I took the chance to do my social butterfly bit, chatting with as many of the gang as I could. Once the music started I would struggle to hear folk. My time working for Scapa Yarns did nothing to improve my dodgy ears. I was grand in normal situations but loud background noise left me struggling to catch what folk were saying which I found really frustrating.

The DJ would end up doing a grand job playing plenty of the old tunes whilst also catering for the many young folk present. Paul must have had a word with the DJ and the next thing I knew I was being pushed onto the dance floor and giving it my all to do a half decent Irish Jig' to the music of *Galway Girl*. Thankfully Sacko joined me with his brilliant take on an exaggerated jig. For some reason folk really enjoyed watching me and Sacko's pathetic efforts. Well gave them a laugh anyway. As Sacks and me wearily made our way back to our seats, the DJ decided to play *Gangnam Style*. I must say, I love that tune and going off the way the dance floor filled, it seems everyone did.

While I sat there catching my breath, I looked to the dance floor to see anyone I recognised. Ste and Dave Lynch were up, Mr Martin Farnworth, Dicky Doran and my old mucker Kenny. At this time, although much improved by the drug Methotrexate, Kenny's knee movements were still pretty restricted. The thing is with Kenny you would never guess it. As I watched my friend dancing with his lovely wife Nicola, all I could see was a guy having a ball and I have never seen the bloke approach life in any other manner. He always give me the impression this fella had life sussed (is that a proper word?).

Daz Smith, who was dancing with his partner at Kenny's side, was another lad I envied. Daz and me were good mates. Life had thrown a few emotional grenades in Daz's path but, as in Kenny's case, Daz chose the optimistic path. It seems some folk, no matter what life throws at them just refuse to stay down for long. Brilliant.

The next thing I knew Dawn was nudging me, pointing in the direction where Mr Leach was dancing with Hazel.

"Look at him, proud as a peacock ha ha. How good a sight is that," I said.

Clad in his new suit, swinging a leg with a bonny lass, Paul had no control over the gormless smile that now furnished his giggling face. Cannot tell you how that sight warmed my belly. A couple of songs later we were treated to the tunes supplied by Paul's recommended Abba tribute group and to be fair they were bloody good. Yes, we all agreed they were mighty fine.

Towards the end of the night our Michael got up to say a few words in the way of thanking Paul for his superb efforts to ensure this night ran like clockwork. Although this tribute was well warranted, Paul was never comfortable in the spotlight. This accounted for his reluctance to agree to a joint celebration for our 60th birthdays the following year, which were only a couple of months apart. I really had to work hard to convince Paul it was a grand idea. Eventually I talked him round, but it was not easy. After another couple of dances on a packed floor in the company of Mick Williams and the equally daft Sacko and Big Bird, everything slowed down along with the slower ballads that were now being played like *Love Can Build a Bridge* by the mother and daughter duo, the Judds. It turned out to be a great night as well as a profitable one, raising around £800 for our club. There were many reluctant farewells bid by folk who had so enjoyed themselves.

The following few weeks passed with Paul and me enjoying the routine we had fallen into. Truth be told, we both enjoyed the simple approach to life we had adopted. While in each other's company, neither of us felt the need to make any effort to fend off the dreaded silences that should have a natural place in communal chats. When you think about it, it's a ridiculous idea that if you are in the company of a mate or mates, then every second must be filled with chatter. Don't get me wrong, there are times many of us can chat for hours on end, but again some people feel uneasy when the inevitable dry ups come around. And yes I can hear our Michael after reading this saying, "My God, there is no one worse than you Eamon for rambling on nonstop". I cannot deny this. In my defence I blame the Irish in me.

What I am trying to say is its grand when you are in the company of someone who enjoys a chat and also is comfortable with silent moments to reflect. Anyway, Paul and me could be sat together for some time without a word passing between us, yet feel comfortable. The bottom line is, this makes life more relaxing. With Paul and me approaching our 60th year of our mostly enjoyable lives, relaxing felt mighty fine. The exciting moments, good and bad, will come along periodically. We will enjoy or deal with them as they arrive.

34.

MR AL KEOWN

One Wednesday afternoon Mr Leach and me were in our usual places outside Costa in the market square.

"How you doing lads?"

"Cor blimey, how ya doin cocker?"

Mick Williams is a mucker from way back. It is always a pleasure to see Willy, he is a cracking lad. Willy's job is caring for mentally and physically challenged kids and, going by a piece in the Bury Times, doing a damn fine job.

"Have you heard about Al Keown?"

"No, What?"

"Well, it seems he has throat cancer and they want to remove his tongue".

"You're joking," I stupidly said.

"No," Paul chipped in, "cannot see Al Keown agreeing to that".

"You are right, neither can I," I said. "Well it seems you are both right, he has refused".

For a moment the three of us just stared at one another, silently thinking the same thing. By refusing the advice of the surgeon it seemed certain to the three of us that Al's chances of survival would be greatly reduced.

"Well, thanks for cheering us up Willy. Have you got any good news?"

"Funny you should ask, keep it to yourselves, I have won half a million on the lottery".

"What? You are joking (there I go again)".

"No. Me, Linda and the kids will be on a world cruise this time next month".

Paul and me were dropped on. "Brilliant. Made up for you cocker."

"I'm sorry lads, felt like I had to cheer you up. Sorry. I cannot believe you would fall for a story like that. Catch ya later lads" and then walked off with a stupid grin on his face.

As kids, mine and Al Keown's paths rarely crossed. The main reason for this was simple; I avoided him. Even as a young lad growing up round the Gigg Lane area of the town, Al's reputation as a trouble causer went before him. I, on the other hand, was a model citizen. Alright, a lad who preferred the quiet life, I would go out of my way to avoid the Al Keown's of this world. As in so many cases, it would be later in life that I would have my assumptions on certain folk overturned. In Mr Keown's case the setting was a communal drink after a funeral. We were paying our respects to the one and only Kenny Catlow.

Kenny was a well-known character round the town. The tales of his exploits in his role as a local referee in the Bury Amateur League are now legendary. If you were unlucky enough to acquire a booking, or even a sending off, it became common knowledge that if you were to call into Kenny's local hostelry the 'Brickcroft' in Freetown, the 'Cotton Tree' on Moorgate or the New Inn and treat Kenny to a couple of pints, well you could sleep soundly in the knowledge the offence would not be reported.

Truth was, Kenny hated the task of filling the forms in. Wisely this was not made common knowledge and ensured Kenny had many a subsidised Saturday night out. After the funeral many of us headed for the Mecca for people of a certain age, the brilliant 'White Lion'. Sat at a table with half a dozen Catlow fans, I settled into comfortable conversation, mostly involving Mr Catlow's character. My comfort ended abruptly when Mr Al Keown took the empty seat at my side. To cut a very long story short, by the time I rose to take my leave, I reluctantly bid farewell for Mr Keown. What a cracking lad! How could I have been so wrong? The answer is simple. I had made the mistake of allowing myself to be influenced by other people's opinions.

Yet another lesson in the school of life. Let no one colour your opinion of anyone, only your own experience. It became a standing joke between Al and me that after each successive funeral and we parted company, one of us would say, "Take care cocker. See you at the next funeral". Sadly it never seems too long between these events.

35.

"OH MR LEACH"

As Christmas 2012 arrived I was hoping to tempt Mr Leach to join me, Dawn and whoever at our table for Christmas dinner. Paul informed me, much as he would like to, for the last couple of years he had joined his brother-in-law Dez and his family for their celebrations. Fair dos! I loved Christmas and in my mind the more the merrier. I made sure any family members on their own were strongly encouraged to join our table and usually many did. With many of us reaching advanced years, these get-togethers were precious and awarded all present with great comfort.

After the New Year celebrations Paul informed me that he and Hazel had arranged a couple of weeks at Paul's tidy apartment at Los Gigantes in Tenerife. The year before Dawn and me had spent a brilliant ten days there in the company of Paul.

"Good on ya cocker. When ya going?"

"Mid June".

"Hazel will love it and it will give you time to get to know each other".

"Hope so" said Paul.

Paul's only complaint concerning Hazel lay in the fact he had had so little quality time with her. "Tell you now Paul, once Hazel is over there at your place, she won't be able to do anything else but relax and enjoy herself".

Two weeks before departure, Paul joined me at our table outside Costa. I could tell immediately from Paul's body language something was wrong. On our numerous long country walks, because the trust was already there, Mr Leach and me shared thoughts I would not even share with family. I reckon this was the reason I always felt the need for a best mate (how childish does that sound). Someone to share your deepest fears and hopes with. Don't get me wrong, the thought of having deep and meaningful talks all the time would be anything but enjoyable, but without doubt there is a place for them, and it must be awful being in a position where you have no trusted outlet.

As a result I know Paul's character almost as well as my own. By his demeanour and body language I knew he was troubled.

"Alright, what's up?"

"She has finished it".

"Who has finished what?"

"Hazel, she wants to make a go of it with her ex".

"Sorry to hear that cocker". I could see Paul was struggling to get his head round this. "To be fair to Hazel Paul, she let you know she was after friendship above all else. The thought of the family together again is a powerful incentive".

"I know, I know, just doesn't make me feel any better".

"I know cocker, no matter how hard it seems now, in time you will be able to move on".

I knew even as I was saying these words to Paul how ineffective they would be. When we are enduring our darkest moments, comforting words from family and friends, sadly, rarely ease the pain of loss. No, there is no quick fix. Only time, and usually plenty of it, provides the balm. It makes you feel so inadequate when someone you love is hurting and you feel powerless to help them.

Those last couple of weeks leading up to what would be a pretty lonesome holiday saw my mate Paul struggle to lift his spirits up to holiday mode. On the Saturday before Paul was to leave for his apartment in Tenerife we kept to our usual routine of a country walk. This time we went up Birtle with my dog Harry and then on to support the lads of Elton Vale. I tried hard to raise my friend's spirits. On the homebound journey with his favourite Big Country CD playing, Paul and me howling along, he seemed relaxed enough. Paul pulled up outside my home on Bury Road.

As I opened the passenger door and climbed out, to my delight Paul did the same and made his way towards me. Our embrace left me very emotional. It was not as if Paul and me didn't have a tactile friendship but without a doubt there was something in that hug.

"Paul, now listen up. You have yourself a good time and do me a favour".

"What's that?"

"Take it easy on the grog".

"Can't promise that cocker, but I will try".

Those were our parting words. Paul always worried me with his drinking, especially so soon after his cancer scare. During the following couple of weeks I received a couple of texts from Paul that went some way to convincing me he was enjoying himself. It seems even in a text you can detect insincerity. Well, he is home Tuesday. His brother Roy was to pick him up at Manchester Airport. This is where fate played her fickle hand.

Dawn my wife was discharged after a major operation on that Tuesday and, although it was frustrating when I was informed Paul had returned unwell with a suspected tummy infection, I needed to be with Dawn and would be unable to get together with Paul for a catch up. I rang Paul on that Wednesday to inform him of this situation.

"No problem Eam. I am off to get some Imodium from Mile Lane Chemist. See you soon".

What can you do? Never mind, shouldn't be too long.

The following day at around 9.30am I was making my way to Breightmet Medical Centre on a visit to see my doctor. As I approached the Mecca Bingo Hall my phone rang. It was Paul's brother-in-law, Dez.

"How you doing cocker?"

"Not brilliant Eamon. Listen. I have got some bad news."

"Don't tell me, Mr Leach is drunk as a monkey and cannot get the key in his door ha ha".

"Eamon, listen it's Paul, he's not going to make it".

"What you on about? Not going to make it?"

The emotion in Dez's voice hit home as he answered me.

"Eamon, Paul's very ill and the doctors don't think he will pull through".

These words cut into me. My breathing became erratic and my chest tightened. As my legs wobbled I flopped onto the low wall around the bingo hall.

"Eamon, you all right?"

By this time my power of speech had deserted me. All I could do was mumble between sobs as Dez was talking away with himself. I was able to grasp his last words.

"When you get the chance, get yourself up to Fairfield Eam".

I couldn't answer Dez, but I knew what I had to do.

I made my way home. God knows what anyone passing me thought. I didn't care anyway. What did it matter? As I stepped in my home Dawn walked into our living room. Immediately Dawn's hand covered her face.

"Oh my God. What's happened?"

My appearance told her something awful. All I managed was, "It's Paul. He's dying".

I then just fell to pieces. "Eamon you have to get up to the hospital now". She then rang our Michael who left work right away and set off for my house. From there we headed up to Fairfield Hospital.

Michael's emotional state snapped me back to the present

enough to warn him to take care over his driving. After arriving at Fairfield we made our way to their ICU Unit. Dez was there and Paul's estranged wife, Karen. After hugging, we discussed what could have possibly brought Paul to this point. I said I didn't understand. He set off for that holiday a fit man. Regular gym visits, regular long country walks. It just doesn't make any sense. We were informed it was thought that Paul had eaten some mussels, which resulted in food poisoning. I could understand that but Paul had a strong constitution even after the cancer, which in itself proved his resistance, and his physical strength was legendary. Many years digging for British Gas only added a little more.

I said, "that wouldn't do it, no way".

Dez informed me, "Eamon he was in bed for nearly a week in 40 degree heat".

First thing that came to me was recalling the fact that the year before while on holiday with Paul, other than a large fan in the main bedroom, his apartment was devoid of air conditioning.

"God, I could only imagine how tough that would have been. What about a doctor?"

"It seems after a couple of visits from folk he was acquainted with in surrounding apartments, he apparently declined the offer of a doctor".

"Yes, but surely as he deteriorated they must have known he needed medical attention".

Dez and Karen fell silent and for a while the four of us just stared at the floor and trying to make sense of all this nonsensical information just confused us more.

I cannot speak for the others but there is no way I was prepared for the sight of my mucker as he lay in that bed with bags and tubes all over his poor ravaged body. I lost it and broke down uncontrollably. Our Michael and me hugged and kissed Paul, whispering private promises in Paul's hopefully receptive ears. Karen telling me to stop snivelling certainly brought me back to myself.

Looking around the ward, it seemed full of very sick folk who hopefully would fare better than my mucker. After reluctantly bidding Paul farewell, we set off to seek solace wherever we could find it. Our Michael came back to mine where we were joined by an equally shell-shocked Kenny Buckle. Dawn was like a fretting mother hen, busying herself making tea, coffee, snacks, whatever while us three lads mumbled lame comments in an attempt to comfort one another.

At around 4pm our Michael received a text from big Dez advising they had just switched the life support off. It just felt like a knife being twisted in my guts. This news left the four of us too upset for words. We needed time to try to take the whole horrible mess in.

It seems at these dreaded times us Kavanaghs seem to derive some sort of perverse comfort from uttering words that we know will cut us to the quick.

I said, "I never told Paul I loved him".

Our Michael and Kenny replied in unison, "Eam, he knew, God's sake. The two of you were never apart".

Then Michael came out with, "me and Paul arranged before his holiday, that when he came back I would be out on the town with him every weekend".

Kenny went on as we listened, "listen folks, let's make a promise to ourselves here and now, we will always talk about Paul like he is still around. To be honest, I like to think he is. The time will come soon enough when we can talk about him without getting choked up".

We knew Kenny was right, but for the time being we needed to grieve. Paul passed away on the 4 July 2013.

The twelve days leading up to the funeral for me personally were peppered with moments of grief that came on unexpectedly and at moments that were to cause me some embarrassment; on a packed bus while stood in the middle of the aisle, also a couple of times on my own sat outside Costa Coffee in the market square whilst staring at the seat where Paul should be sat going on with himself. Very few people escape experiencing deep grief over the passing of a loved one, sadly this fact is of no help whatsoever when you are facing it. Sometimes while on my own, I found myself so angry at Paul for not seeking medical help sooner. I need my mucker back.

Shouting as if he were there, "what were you thinking of Mr Leach. Why? Why?" It takes time. It is so true. Time alone is the balm. Ageing in most aspects of life brings more contentment, each and every experience gifts you more wisdom, good or bad. Alas, each soul I lose, of which there have been many, is just as deeply felt as the first. The upside is contained in your reinvigorated love of life and taking nothing for granted.

A few months later I received a call from my newish buddy, Al Keown. "Just thought I would let you know I have been given the all clear".

"Oh my God Al, cannot tell you how happy that makes me".

"Cheer's cocker".

I arranged to go down to Al's the following evening. The next day saw me sat with Al in the kitchen of his Radcliffe Road home, chatting over our cups of tea. I had to laugh when this lad in front of me, with the previous reputation compared to an old Western gunslinger said, "this health shock has really affected me Eam"

"How do you mean?"

"Put it this way, I get emotional over coffee adverts".

"Ha, ha get away".

"Come on, you know what I mean".

All I could think was that in a strange way this awful event would end up being a blessing to this witty, moody madman with his wicked sense of humour. As I rose to take my leave I said to Al, "Tell you one thing cocker, your decision to not allow the surgeon to remove your tongue has got to be the best decision you will make in your life".

A heartfelt hug and I was out the door.

This would be a time where I guess I was spending too much time in my own head. Not really fair to those around you. I made a promise to make a concerted effort to reach a conclusion concerning the events leading up to Paul's passing. I just knew I would never be able to quiet my enquiring mind. After spending a full week of free time going over the facts, I came to a conclusion that I was 95 per cent sure was accurate.

I knew once settled into holiday mode in his apartment, Paul on each night on the town would be consuming large amounts of alcohol. Add to this his compromised immune system. Well along with 40º heat and no air-conditioning, it is no surprise that after a tummy infection he ended up in a state. The connection between mental health and physical health is well documented. I cannot even bare to spend too long thinking of Paul in this awful situation. How he made the arduous journey home I will never know.

My old mucker has his permanent place in my heart, along with my collection of family and friends no longer physically with us. I apologise if I have depressed you readers. The truth is that along with the good times will always be the testing low times. This is life as it has always been. A massive thank you to Paul Mills (Millsy) for his thoughtful accolade at Paul's funeral which included many comical tales of his life.

"Well done cocker".

36.

IN PRAISE OF HEROES

Ever since I can remember I have taken great enjoyment in attending the Annual Remembrance Sunday parade. Joining the ranks of what seems to be most of the population of Bury gathering in the centre. Me and my brother Michael usually meet outside the Robert Peel. There is a narrow ginnel running the full length from the Robert Peel to Wilds on the corner of Bolton Street. There is just enough room for one body at a time to pass through. Due to our lack of height Michael and me struggled to get a view of proceedings. Over the years our kid and me struck up a friendship with three old soldiers. Feels almost like the cue for a joke, as one was a sailor, one an RAF man and the other a regular soldier. We all stand around, as if to attention, adhering to the minute's silence. During the whole parade, from start until we set off for home, you can feel pride welling up in your gut, settling somewhere in the chest area.

It makes me think of the comradeship and community feeling that, sadly, only seems to flourish during a time of war. These situations in modern life are so rare. Our lives have become so insular now that there is little real community in Britain. The people who congregate in Bury on this special occasion finally find an outlet for all their suppressed feelings of pride and community. The fact is you can sense the emotion of the folk around you reaching a level where they can hardly contain it. It is truly a special time. It is so unique for so many folk to be gathered to pay respects to the lads and girls who made the ultimate sacrifices so you and me can roam free and speak our minds.

We look back as older folk and remember how it was when we were younger. We have had a taste of how life can be and we sure do miss it.

When the parade comes to an end, our kid and me seek refreshment within the walls of the Robert Peel (Wetherspoons). On entering we would seek out our friends, the three servicemen. Jim, Pat and Tommy sat together discussing the events of the day. After taking their order, our kid and me took great pride in keeping the pints coming for these grand old fellas. They must have found it comical the way me and our kid hung on to every word they uttered and were probably a little over eager to carry out any request the lads asked. The three of them at this time were frail with age. Sadly the last of our trio, Tommy, passed on a couple of years ago. I can honestly say we will miss them. Our kid, health permitting, and me will never miss a Remembrance Sunday. Who in their right mind would miss an experience that fills you with a mixture of love and pride?

One Tuesday in November, as usual I had met my older brother Pat at Big Jim's Café. I have always enjoyed our Pat's company. He is a very wise old sage and one of the few practicing Catholics I know. He also possesses a wicked sense of humour. This combination I think makes him a special man. Anyway, after parting, I headed for the bus stop on Bolton Street. To my real surprise large crowds were gathering around the junction of Market Street and The Rock. On asking a lady what was happening, she replied, "Don't you know? Our boys are back from Afghanistan".

"Blimey," I said, "it cannot be common knowledge, no one has mentioned it".

"Well," she said, "they are due any minute".

"Brilliant," I thought and secured a place for myself. It was not long before we caught the military music of marching boots. The anticipation flooded all of us gathered there. Another minute and the fabulous sight of our superbly turned out soldiers, arms swinging in perfect time with their feet came into view.

I, along with the rest of the now large crowd, came over very emotional. Many gave voice to their pent up feelings with shouts of, "You make us proud". "Heroes". "Well done lads", together with enthusiastic clapping, resulted in tears flooding my eyes. Someone patted me on the back.

"You all right Eam?"

I turned and stared into the tear-stained face of my mate Tony Stockholm. Instantly we burst out laughing at the sight of each other.

"Cannot help it Eam. You just get caught up in the emotion. Great isn't it ha ha".

37.

BURY MARKET

Bury Market has always been a special place, from the days of the old market right up to the present day. It has always held a place in the hearts of Buryites. We owe the person who created the black pudding for forcing the name Bury into worldwide consciousness. Maybe worldwide is a bit strong, but only a bit. Robert Peel was a man who anyone would take pride in and Bury FC still holds the record for most goals scored in an FA Cup Final. But for me, it is not any of these enviable achievements that draw folk from far and wide. I reckon there is a quality in the makeup of your average Buryite. That is unique in its tolerance, warmth and genuine approach to life. Paul and me saw it on a weekly basis. Twenty, thirty coaches each market day, full of folk from Liverpool, Blackpool, Cumbria, Yorkshire and too many other places to name here. We have had folks from all these places and many more sat with us at Big Jims. They all seem to enjoy a chat with the locals as much as the many bargains they can buy on Bury Market.

Paul and me and other members of the brew gang got to know some of these visitors so well they have now become friends. Sharing other folk's thoughts and views is such a healthy pastime. It stops you getting too preoccupied with yourself. I have helped a few friends out on their stalls on the outside market. Reg runs the 'Coffee Pot Café'. I was comfortable with my job of clearing tables and washing up. Things got too stressful when Reg asked me to cook and do the counter. Okay with one or two folk waiting to be served but a big queue and I froze. See you Reg!

Ian ran a handbag and suitcase stall facing Reg's Cafe. He also had a greeting card shop next to his bag stall. One day Ian came to collect his takings. Embarrassed I had to inform Ian, in eight hours I had not sold one bag. To his credit he tried me on his card stall. Alas no better at that. At least now I know if I had to make a living selling, I would starve.

While working on the outside market I got to know many of the stall holders and a cracking lot they are. When I shop at their stalls they always knock a bit off. Lovely. Our Pat and I have been patronising Big Jim's for at least thirty years. The workforce has changed but thankfully they always seem to hire lovely thoughtful girls. Julie, the Manageress runs a tight ship. We all love Michelle. She has been there forever, plus she is very attentive. Sometimes you are lucky to get a seat. It has really helped now they have extended. It was not lost on Paul and I how lucky we were. Tuesdays walking, Wednesdays and Fridays the cafe gang, Saturdays walking in the morning, afternoons footy at the Vale. Just as well my wife Dawn is the understanding kind. She loved Paul and kept herself busy with her own friends and interests. She also insists we have some quality time together, which we do and, fingers crossed, everything is "hunky dory".

38.

THE SHAKERS

By no stretch of the imagination could anyone call me a dedicated, loyal fan of Bury FC. Some of the reasons for this are obvious. I played footy every Saturday, varying standards, various leagues and too many teams to list here. But if the situation presented itself and a couple of muckers were up for it, we paid homage. I had some very emotional times at Gigg.

From the 1960s to the present, each decade was punctuated with drama, either fighting off relegation or pushing for promotion. Plus each decade gifted Bury supporters with some great characters. The 60s for Bury talent has to be our golden years. To name but a few: Colin Bell, Bill Calder, Bobby Collins, Alec Lindsay, Jimmy Kerr and my old mucker George Jones. The decades that followed were peppered with magical moments provided by individuals gifted with so much talent they could influence results on their own. In 1972 I was one of a large crowd gathered at Gigg Lane to entertain our illustrious neighbours Manchester City in the League Cup. It was a Tuesday night and there was magic in the air. The very air itself was tingling with hope and fear. As this will be a personal view, make allowances for factual errors. A young Scot came in at full-back for Bury. One Vic Doherty. The City side contained their classic Bell, Lee and Summerbee. All I remember is that the boys and me were as high as kites willing the lads on, and on they went! John Murray put us 1–0 up.

By this time I was having trouble with my breathing. Unbelievably we then went 2–0 up.

"Oh my God, please don't let City score".

Young Vic was doing a grand job, almost snuffed Lee out completely. I think it was George Hamstead got the second that sent us Bury fans into ecstasy. As George beckoned the crowd to increase our vocal support, the rallying cry did not go unheeded. Making up half the 16,000 crowd, each of us felt personally involved in every pass, tackle, shot and save. What a night, brilliant!

As me and the boys knew sleep would evade us that night, we headed for Alfred Street to chat until the wee hours dissecting the game, picking out high points of which there were many. Not even worried about how knackered we would be the next day. The work at Antlers did not demand too much concentration. Just as well.

39.

LOCAL HEROES

In the early days on the sporting front my own choice would be the Bury FC midfielder Jimmy Kerr. What a player. I used to watch this great Scotsman and try to model myself on him. The man was a joy to behold. It seemed to me his mum must have given birth to the lad and from then on made sure a ball accompanied him wherever he was. The ball appeared to be just as extension of his body. So natural. So sad. After leaving Bury for Blackburn Rovers, Jimmy broke his leg badly and sadly never recovered his full potential.

I always admired Bury's full-back Hugh Tinney. Apart from being a bloody good full-back, he attended the same church as myself. I found it heart-warming, as daft as this sounds, to witness a fella I had paid to watch playing football sitting in front of me in church and on his knees paying homage to God. Another fella I would class as a personal hero would be my PE teacher at St Gabriel's, Mick Tonge. His enthusiasm was so infectious. Mr Tonge and, to a lesser extent, Mr Richmond added magic to our regular PE lessons. Mick was skilled in the psychological side of the game, recognised each player's strengths and weaknesses and took time out to work on those weaknesses. Put simply, he made us better players.

Robert Peel must go down as Bury's most famous son. Mill owner, land owner, Prime Minister, who then went on to form an organised police force. The story I was told as a child, concerning his fabulous statue that graces the market place, many of you will recognise, it is the one concerning his waistcoat; namely it being buttoned up on the wrong side. The tale goes on to report that the sculptor involved killed himself because of this massive error. A sad tale, but alas a false tale. The truth turns out to be a little more benign. It seems the talented Mr Peel had damaged the fingers on one hand and found it easier to have his buttons on his left side.

'Altruism' to me is such a precious quality. The Kay's, a family that I read about recently impress me so much. The Byroms of Tottington, going back to James in the mid-1800s pulled himself up by his breeches. Born to poor working class folk this plucky fella steadily built up his small building firm to the extent where it became a hugely successful countrywide concern. A devout Wesleyan, after erecting a whole street to be named Byrom Street, he, his sons and their sons either built, repaired, extended or improved half the buildings in our fair town. To their credit they always helped those less fortunate.

40.

CHURCH

Christmas day 2013 found me in the company of my wife Dawn, her daughter Tanya and her partner Kelly, both absolute darlings. We had all opened our presents and had our breakfast. To my surprise my mind became flooded with a powerful compulsion to be inside a church. A couple of years before a church had opened its doors in a building that was previously occupied by a company called Homespare on the small Boundary Industrial Estate across from my home. I must admit I was curious as to the persuasion this church lent itself to. A couple of weeks before I needed to call at 'George Hills' woodyard, a few yards down from the church and I decided to enquire at this so called "Kings Church". The gentleman who answered the rear door was happy to inform me Kings Church was a free church, leaning towards Evangelical. This gave me a vague idea of how proceedings would pan out.

So forward to Christmas Day and my mysterious longing to satisfy what seemed a spiritual calling. Looking out of my front window across the busy A58 I noticed a trickle of casually but smartly dressed folk heading in the direction of Kings Church. Absentmindedly I uttered the words, "That's it, I am off to church".

"I think I will join you," said Kelly. I was glad to hear it. It is always nicer to have company on an adventure.

"Right Kelly get ya glad rags on".

Twenty minutes later Kelly and me joined a group of folk passing through the church door into a spacious foyer full of people, some in a casual uniform with the words 'Kings Giants' written on their tops. What this referred to as yet I knew not. What surprised Kelly and me initially was that not one person passed us without a warm honest greeting. We made our way slowly towards the entrance to a huge hall. As we entered this hall Kelly and me ended up just staring at one another with gormless grins on our faces. No idea what I was expecting but wow, at the far end of this hall was a raised stage. On this stage were a collection of young lads and girls busying themselves with either tuning guitars, setting drums up and adjusting mics. The fabulous sight topping this was the hall at this time already contained around a couple of hundred people of all ages, all sizes, all colours greeting each other in a way normally restricted to immediately family.

Kelly whispered something to me that will stay with me forever as it captured the emotion we were both feeling. "You can feel the love" and it was true. Watching these folk interacting with each other was nothing short of beautiful. You just knew there was no pretence here. No feigned niceties, these folk were totally focused on everyone but themselves. There was something about them that words cannot express and had Kelly and me feeling like intruders. Intruders who to be honest were envious of these folk. Why we felt this way was a mystery as we could not have been more warmly welcomed.

On a large screen positioned behind the young folk on the stage was a digital clock counting the seconds down to 10.30am. As the allotted time approached the undisguised excitement was tangible. The group on stage were prepared and as 10.30 struck they burst into the intro of a song that, while it lent itself to religious preaching, was so damn catchy. Any resistance to joining in was immediately forgotten. Even so Kelly and me were thankful the words to this brilliant song were displayed on the screen so all who needed to could follow.

Amongst us in the huge congregation were many teenagers who were literally bouncing up and down, arms in the air, completely lost in what could only be described as happiness. The older folk were not to be outdone. It seemed no one was able to keep their limbs still for any length of time. Kelly and me, still feeling a little self-conscious, were gently swaying from side to side, occasionally giving each other smiling sideways glances. Yes, we were really enjoying the proceedings. There followed more high-energy music and songs. The breaks between songs were taken up with positive chats involving the audience on the joy of a common goal. You could not help but get caught up in the emotion radiating from so many folk expressing their joy of just being alive and being together celebrating the God they all love. Even in what they considered a broken world.

We were then treated to a very informative talk by a fella called Derek. I personally found Derek's talk nothing short of a revelation. I so wished I had a tape of it. The simplistic way he spoke of his belief, incredibly using humour to emphasise certain points, taking the congregation through a comical story in which, because of their Christian faith, wherever and whatever situation they found themselves in they could bring light to the folk who seem lost in the darkness.

I know this sounds corny, but that's down to my failure to express and capture the quality and power of Derek's words. I honestly found it inspirational and really did not want it to end. Young Kelly and I were finding this whole experience so uplifting. I was still digesting Derek's words when the band that included three guitars, drums and two bonny young lasses on vocals who both had fabulous voices, began to play. As the service came to an end, Kelly and me reluctantly made our way out of the great hall. Our progress was very slow as we never advanced more than a couple of yards without folk greeting us shaking our hands and genuinely wanting us to stay around. As Dawn had texted Kelly to say our dinners were on the table, we made our way home. Cannot speak for Kelly, but my first visit to "Kings Church" had a massive effect on me. To be in a room with around three hundred folk of every possible variety and instinctively sense it's a room full of pure love, well it's just so special.

I know what some of you will be thinking. But it was not just me, Kelly felt the same. These occasions are normally so rare. I remember a couple of years back me and Dawn attended the Manchester 10K charity run. Tanya and her partner at the time, Vicky were taking part. The highlight for Dawn and me was that the whole atmosphere was totally positive. It has happened a couple of times when I have been watching Bury FC but not very often and not as powerfully. These rare occasions make you feel so damn good. In a world that seems to lack the spiritual benefits of strong communities they are literally a Godsend. As we get older we tend to spend more time pondering the big questions, and isn't it life affirming when some of them are answered.

41.

LEO

Here I am. Friday 1pm sat outside Costa Coffee. It has been several months now since Paul passed on. In truth I was in low spirits, really missing the little bugger. I engage in social niceties with passing folk. Its okay, just not the same. It's nobody's fault. All my muckers are working. That was the beauty of mine and Paul's situation. No longer wage slaves, literally 'free men'.

An hour gone and I have not exchanged more than a couple of words. By this time there is just me and another fella sat a table away from me. He seems to be engrossed in making notes onto a pad he was holding with a certain reverence. He was a big fella, but to be fair he had the build of a chap who regularly worked out. In what form I could only guess. As this chap seemed to be really concentrating on the notes he was making, I took the chance to check him out. Oh my God, no, it cannot be, if this chaps not David Glossop, it's his bloody twin. This is always a tricky situation. The guy may not welcome an intrusion. Bugger it, I'm too curious.

"Excuse me, do you mind if I ask you something".

"No, fire away".

"Do you know a lad called David Glossop?"

"He's my much older brother".

Music to my ears, in that one sentence this lad had not only answered my question but also let me know he owned a brilliant sense of humour.

"Knew it, you are a dead ringer".

"We are identical twins. Just happened I proved a long labour, ten years in fact. Ha ha". Turns out his name is Leo.

The next hour was taken up with, as the song goes, *Getting to Know You*. Turns out Leo is a retired policeman. Bingo! Asking him if he was writing a book, he informed me he was attempting to learn Italian. This impressed me no end as I had always fancied learning another language. However, I was also repeatedly told to master English first. Point taken. I knew a little about Leo's family. I was a friend of his brother David through all our school days. In the sixties and seventies the Glossops ran a butcher's shop in the fish and meat market. I also knew they hailed from the Walmersley area of the town and his sister Celia's beauty attracted many admiring glances. So Leo and me entered into a friendship that, speaking personally, is good and solid.

Silly as it seems, initially I carried a feeling of guilt. A feeling I was being unfaithful to Paul's memory. It took a little while but I eventually realised if Mr Leach was looking down on me during those doubting thoughts, his words to me would be, "Eamon you will be joining me soon enough. Get on with it man". And God knows he could be right. So now poor Leo on Wednesdays and Fridays has to listen to the moronic ramblings of a plastic Irishman who, for some reason, believes he has lived long enough to assume he has opinions with enough insight to be deemed interesting. The great thing with Leo is he spends a lot of time correcting my many wrong assumptions. I am not the sort of fella to begrudge being corrected. Leo for his age is a wise chap. I would be a fool not to let myself be informed. To be brutally honest we spend the bulk of our time talking absolute rubbish and the fact is it suits us both fine. During our chats Leo enjoys partaking of a huge Havana cigar. Not saying they are long, but the first half he used a rod rest. Like myself Leo keeps himself occupied, seeing this as a healthy approach to life, and enjoys visits to the gym, several nights playing squash and keeping his home in order as well as reading and occasional visits to a local hostelry.

As for myself, more and more of my time is spent in the company of the members of my family who are experiencing ill health. Up until lately – even though a couple of us have had what you could consider serious health problems – in truth they have not proved too disruptive. My folks are strong believers in 'getting on with it'. At this moment in time it turns out I am the only able bodied Kavanagh male available. Our John's arthritis is so severe he rarely leaves his flat. So before I meet Leo I shop for whatever John tells me he needs, spend a couple of hours watching the greatest woman on the planet (Judge Judy) or a western. Our John has never been one for idle chat. He seems well happy being master of his remote and an occasional visit from his brothers suits him fine.

Our Pat has just been diagnosed with Parkinson's, which came as no big surprise to the family. Patrick was displaying many of the symptoms of this disease. I help Pat with his large rear garden, which I have to admit I enjoy. So enjoy our Pat's company. I was made up when he agreed to meet me at Big Jim's on Tuesdays at, you guessed it, 1 pm.

Our Sheila has recently moved back to old Blighty from Spain. Ramsbottom to be exact. I have spent quite a bit of time lending a hand where I can to make a presentable home.

As our dog Harry happens to be a bundle of energy, I make sure soon as I have had my breakfast, we are in the backyard. Me sat at one end holding two rubber balls, Harry at my side practically levitating with excitement, waiting for me to chuck one of the balls. The reason I need two balls lies in the fact Harry has never cottoned on to how the game is played. If I was not holding another ball he simply would not release the one in his mouth. As my yard is a good fifteen yards in length, after around an hour, Harry along with my right arm begins to tire.

Our outings to the countryside near my home over the last couple of years have become hazardous what with the paths strewn with dog muck and young lads out with dogs. Well, if Harry did not contract some disease, chances are he would be torn apart by one of these idiot's unleashed trophy dogs. Weekends are Harry's extra exciting times when my mucker Mr Buckle drives me and Harry to greener and more pleasant beauty spots for the three of us to enjoy a morning's walk.

Lately in order to give Harry more to think about I have started throwing three balls. Watching his over excited confusion, with Harry unable to decide which ball to return to me first, has me in fits of laughter. He will grab a ball, see another, drop the one he has, pick another up, drop that, pick another. So as well as me being entertained for an hour, Harry in the late evening enjoys such a deep sleep, dreaming his dreams, interrupted only by little yelps that always provoke endearing responses from me and Dawn. The sight of Harry and our aged cat Patch curled up together for the night gives the two of us a warm feeling in our bellies to go to bed with.

Me and Leo outside Costa!

42.

BIRDSONG

I have just finished reading Sebastian Faulk's fabulous book, Birdsong. It blew me away. Some writers are so gifted they somehow manage to have you so entranced with proceedings you actually feel part of the story. I was carried along in the company of a young fella who, to say the least, had a rough childhood. This lad worked hard, probably as much to distract his mind as acquiring degrees. Stephen was around nineteen when war broke out in 1914. As became the norm, many of these well-educated young lads were appointed as officers. You can imagine this situation creating friction with some of the lads. As so often happens, the horrors that followed either made them or broke them. Stephen, along the majority of our able bodied men, would witness scenes that no man or woman should ever have to endure. Each man had to find his coping mechanism. Those who failed went under, either ending up nervous wrecks or, even worse, descended into madness. As in life in general, the lads who somehow managed to retain a sense of humour while living through hell became for many others a literal Godsend and keepers of their sanity.

We Buryites have so much to be proud of, Bury being the spiritual and physical home of, as far as I and many others are concerned, the bravest proud men that were, still are, and should always remain the fabulous 'Lancashire Fusiliers'.

Six VC's before breakfast in the slaughter hole of Gallipoli. Does not come any better than these lads. Kids should be informed at school just what they owe to their Granddads and Great-Granddads.

It is unbelievable that the majority of young folk have no concept of the debt owed to the generations of the war years. Ironically, you would think the austere times we are now living through would make people want to create a favourable situation in order to encourage the 'we are all in it together' community feelings of the war years.

Sadly, if anything we have grown more insular. I struggle to understand the reasons for this. It does not make sense. Most of the folk I know really enjoy sharing and lending a hand and truly appreciate the positive enriching responses they receive in return. It seems people living in a loving community environment are becoming an enviable rarity. So it seems the high quality of life that is nurtured by a healthy loving community needs a war to give it birth. What a horrible thought.

It is so frustrating when you think how little effort it takes to improve our environment. Warm greetings to friends and strangers alike. Actually listening, when someone needs to be heard. And remember hugs are so special. A two way gift. Not the ones you see many schoolgirls performing where they are more concerned by who is watching. Quite comical really. Listen to me! Who do I think I am? Well, I have reached an age where if I have not learned the really important things in life then that would be a real worry. Reluctantly I confess the Beatles gave the world its most important message. Enshrined in the words of their song *All you need is love*. I used to get p****d off with almost every song I heard, all concerned with this one subject. But I certainly have changed my mind now. We need it more than ever before. I love the message Bernard Adams of Malvern College imparted to his fellow officers. The only way to run a company is by love, by looking after your men in the trenches by giving them cigarettes and smiles. For a nation still entrenched in class distinctions, I found this heart-warming and reassuring.

43.

THE PROMISED LAND

It seems over the last couple of decades our green and pleasant land has become a magnet for folk from distant lands. In itself no problem, who can blame these folk? I am sure if me or you found every day a struggle just to survive and someone informed us that in Britain they will find you a home and even if have no work they will give you enough to live at a decent standard we would be tempted. Well, what would we say?

"Get me over there, that is the Promised Land".

No, the problem lies with the consecutive Government and party's pathetic attitude to our border control and their approach to immigration. They will tell you we are in the EU, which means freedom of labour and settlement. Well pardon me, knowing our benefit system, where would you or anyone else be heading for? Any folk who have been here for generations cannot help but have noticed the massive effect on our social landscape. This country is, and has been for quite a while, struggling to feed and find work for its mushrooming population.

I find it hard to conceal my anger at these spineless politicians who have turned a blind eye to the obvious problems that the mixture of scarcity of work and paying your rent or mortgage will bring. Why would they worry? They are tucked away in their leafy suburban homes, shielded from the common folk's harsh realities. Food banks, child poverty, God's sake! Well it's the ruling parties, each in their turn, who have lost any sense of BALANCE. It has to be addressed and not by a nation that has been cowed to the point of being afraid to fly our own flag for 'God's sake'.

An example for you Barry Evans, landlord of the 'Derby Arms' on Bolton Road decided as a patriot to adorn the gable end of his popular pub with our national flag. You just know don't you? Yes, within days Barry received a letter from his brewery telling him he must have our flag painted over as some minorities could be offended. I know, beggars belief. Well to Barry's credit he ignored this stupid letter. This country has a fabulous history. Okay, some of it is steeped in harsh treatment of other folk but you have to consider the times they were set in. Political Correctness was unheard of and, to be fair, do not visit the crimes of their forefathers on their sons. The last word on this subject: if you find a party you think may have the 'balls' to instigate change, for God's sake vote for them. And finally, I know sorry! Wouldn't it be grand for good old 'COMMON SENSE' to be the deciding factor when making decisions that will ultimately affect people's lives instead of nonsensical laws?

My fear is folk have been let down so often by our government, there is a chance that the social disease, apathy, will become ingrained it will set to rest the future hope of reclaiming good, time honoured values that enrich any community.

44.

FAB MUSIC

November 1977 finds me working at Scapa yarns, the mill at the back of the Brewers Arms pub. My workmate Michael and I have just finished our 6am – 2pm shift.

"Eamon do you fancy a run to Manchester?"

"Yeah, why not. Always enjoy a trip to the big city".

Usually take the train from Bury. I must admit, Michael's newish Ford Capri waiting in the car park looked very inviting.

As we joined the motorway, Michael said, "fancy some music?" Strangely up to this time I had never rode in a car with music on board. Brilliant.

"Don't suppose you have any country tapes".

"No, but you might enjoy this".

In went the tape and my ears were assaulted by the dynamic intro to *Bat Out of Hell* by Meat Loaf. Literally took my breath away. As the tracks came and went, each one as fabulous as the other, we came to the track *Two out of Three Ain't Bad*. I kid you not; this track fetched me dangerously close to tears. What an absolutely beautiful song. I don't think I spoke a word to Michael all through the album. I caught him having a sneaky giggle occasionally, obviously tickled by my reaction that was to me nothing short of a revelation. The thing is, up to this time, the bulk of my collection was country and Irish. The sort of music I had just listened to was alien to me. All I know is I had been listening to something very special. This was the album that convinced me you should never shut your ears to any music merely because it does not fall into your normal taste. My first words to Michael after the last track were, "any chance we can call in to the record shop on Market Street? I have got to have this album."

Giggling, Michael said, "I take it you enjoyed that Eamon".

Smiling I replied, "what do you think?"

As you can guess, music is very important to me. What made this event with Michael in his car so special was the fact that by this time I had acquired many albums and very rarely did I not really enjoy them. The difference here was the fact every single track blew me away. This was the first time this had happened. As a result, this album will remain so special to me as long as I live.

It has happened since, to a lesser extent. Next were *Glen Campbell's Greatest Hits, Johnny Cash at Folsom Prison,* Bobby Bare, *Lullabies Legends and Lies* and a group I saw live at the Empire Pool, Wembley in 1975 Tompall and the Glazer Brothers. When you think how long I have been collecting music, well you can see it is a rare event. I have been experiencing a worrying trait lately for a guy who considers himself more or less a 'good old boy'; I have taken to really enjoying certain rap artists. This would be considered sacrilegious in some quarters, but as I have already said, we should never close our ears to anything they are enjoying.

Lately my control over my diabetes has not been what it should be. As a result, it has forced me to exercise each evening in order for me to keep my blood sugars at a decent level. I alternate between boxing while listening to a sixties CD; box for one record, rest for one record and so on. My other fitness training is carried out on a very dated exercise bike acquired from my old friend on the next block, Renie. Renie is now 87 years old and, believe it or not, it's only just over a year and a half since she ceased using it and only then after a fall that damaged her hip.

I adopt the same script with the bike as the boxing. Pedal for one track; rest for one, and so on. Obviously it is all good stuff for maintaining my fitness but, as you would expect, I have times when

I would so love to treat myself to fish and chips and a chill out night but since my doctor informed me about the danger of retiring to bed with high sugar levels, well, I suppose within the bigger picture it is a small price.

It seems to me the only exception to my musical deviations is jazz and blues. This proved a slight problem last year when an old girl-friend from my Alfred Street gang days, Christine Dell contacted me via email to inform me she would be returning to Bury for a reunion with her sister Angela and her boyfriend Ged Wilson, a Lowercroft lad. Ged happened to be a very talented acoustic blues artist. We arranged to meet up, along with Christine's husband Andy, at the Automatic Restaurant on Market Street. Christine and me had an hour or so to catch up, which I must say I so enjoyed. During our time as teenagers Christine and me became very close. She informed me I was her first proper boyfriend, which I have to admit, made me feel quite honoured.

In common with most of us, Christine's life has been a mixture of highs and lows. With two children in tow from a previous marriage, fate played her sweet hand when she met up with a chap called Andy. With both of them possessing strong religious beliefs, this added instant stability to their blossoming relationship. After their marriage they were blessed with a little girl. Their hearts were broken when their daughter passed away at the age of seven. I can hardly comprehend the pain this terrible event caused. They were later gifted a son who is now at university. Through all this Christine, to my amazement, still retains a zany childlike approach to life and her hubby Andy is a top man who loves his step-kids as his own. As Ged was appearing at Bury Met to get to his gig we only had to make our way next door.

Now, as I was saying earlier, the one genre of music that least appeals to me happens to be blues and jazz. So as we settled ourselves into our seats, our Michael gracing us with his presence, I confess I felt I was in a tricky situation. The thing was, I felt I would be expected to show enthusiasm for Ged's performance which is natural, only I was a little worried my true feelings would show through.

Well, to Ged's credit, he has come closer than anyone to entice me to be a fan. The lad's energy and enthusiasm are very infectious. As a musician he is without doubt brilliant. Now, I have not become a jazz fan but I have become a Ged Wilson fan. It really was a grand way to finish off a magic day. I walked Ged, Angela, Christine and Andy to their cars that were parked down by the 'Trackside Pub' off Bolton Street. After hugs and bidding them farewell I made my way home.

Michelle, Wendy and Julie at Big Jims

45.

LUCKY MAN

A heart attack in 2003; diagnosed diabetic in 2010. Not everybody's idea of a lucky man but I assure you, I am. Truth is 90 per cent of the time I feel mighty fine. No longer governed by the alarm clock, my time is my own. I wake each morning and my first act is to give thanks for being blessed with another day. Another day to spend in the company of friends and family and very often folk I have never met before. My wife Dawn's health problems are severe by any standards. Cancer has had a severe effect on her quality of life. To her credit and my peace of mind, she is a trooper. We are both well aware that compared to some folk we have no right to moan. I no longer worry about problems that may be skulking in the unpredictable future. As my old mucker Jack once said, "Eamon, don't build bridges before you reach the river". What a wise man he was. I know this will sound corny to many of you, but some days I feel so good I end up feeling euphoric to the point I know I sometimes become a pain to some folk. I need to try to remember that just because I am having one of those days, where for some reason my senses are heightened, it does not follow even though I tend to assume so, that all around me are feeling the same. I need to realise some folk, for whatever reason, are having a shite day. I recently had this fact brought home to me in a way that would cure my naive assumption.

One market day recently I arrived at Big Jim's a little earlier than normal. After acquiring my usual cuppa, I made my way to the only vacant seat, tucked away in the far corner facing the chicken stall. Next to me was a large chap that, at a guess, was in his early seventies. He seemed far away, staring into the middle distance. I should have sensed something was amiss. Alas, here goes.

"How ya doing?"

Nothing. Assuming he was deaf, I touched his knee saying, "You okay?"

These words left his mouth. "Do I f*****g look ok?"

I was dropped on and judging by the reactions of the folk sat near us, I wasn't the only one.

"I am sorry, I didn't mean any offence".

Feeling pretty embarrassed I rose to hopefully find another seat. As I bent to pick up my holdalls I knocked his cup of coffee over. After hitting the floor it splashed onto his shoes and the bottom of his pants.

"Oh my God".

I felt like doing a runner.

"You did that on purpose".

"Trust me, it was an accident, stay there I will get you another brew and a cloth to clean up".

"Don't bother. Just wanted a quiet brew, till you come along, that was what I was having. Tell you what pal, you are an interfering prick."

"I am so sorry".

"Just get out mi way, you idiot".

"Don't be so bloody minded, I saw what happened, it was an accident".

"I know Eamon, there is no way he would be so petty".

I was so thankful for this lady's words. As you can imagine I did not hang around long after asking Julie the cafe manageress to let the brew gang know I would be absent today.

Truth was this incident had really upset me. I decided I needed to be alone to get my confusion sorted. Five minutes later I was in the queue at Costa ordering my usual medium cappuccino. I took a seat at the far end table and sat down with my troubled thoughts. The thing is I hated the thought I had really upset this chap. All right, he was not the most agreeable fella I had ever met, but that is irrelevant.

Lost in my thoughts I failed to notice that someone had sat down on the other chair at my table. Oh God, sat in front of me was the chap from the cafe. My mind racing I mumbled, "I'm so sorry".

"Just go get me a coffee, a plain old coffee, not a tarted up version".

"Course, won't be long".

As I pushed the door open I was greeted by an even longer queue than normal. If you like your Costa you have to cultivate a very patient attitude. Sean the manager, one of life's more colourful characters, what with his impromptu renditions of popular songs and general zany behaviour, was clearing a table at my side.

"Sean, I know you are busy, wouldn't ask, but please, please could you get me a plain white coffee ASAP?"

I reckon Sean sensed my desperation. Two minutes later Sean returned with the coffee.

"Sean, I could kiss you".

"Does it look like I'd mind?"

"Actually no, must get this coffee to this fella".

I very cautiously placed the cup of coffee in front of this chap and just as cautiously sat down facing him. Reluctant to say anything in case I upset him, I just sat there attempting to be amiable while silent (not easy).

"Listen, I have probably had the worse day I have ever had". Then silence. The chap was not attempting to drink his coffee. He was again into staring into the middle distance, as he was when I first set eyes on him.

"Do you mind if I ask your name?" I said.

"Eamon, Eamon Kelly".

For a while I just stared at him, thinking he was winding me up. He'd obviously caught my name at Big Jims. I didn't feel confident enough to test his patience. So in the safety of the truth I replied, "Eamon, can another Eamon shake your hand". With my hand outstretched it tickled me to see the confusion on my namesake's face. What a picture! "Eamon Kavanagh at your service".

Eamon complied a little reluctantly. After showing him my driving licence I think he was convinced. As you can imagine, the next half hour or so was spent chatting about our Irish connections and obviously the incredible coincidence concerning

our first names. It was when Eamon rose to take his leave, stick in hand; he finally broached the subject of what passed in Big Jims.

Costa crew, Shaun (manger), Clare, Stuart, Becky, Richard, Daria

"Listen Eamon I apologise for the way I was with you in there. My wife has advanced dementia. Trust me, it is heart breaking to see my Mrs disappearing a little more each day. Well, my doctor informed me today I have inoperable lung cancer".

Involuntary tears immediately trickled down my cheeks. "God Eamon I am so sorry".

"Don't bother yourself lad, but you understand my frustration now".

"Eamon if our roles had been reversed I would probably have slugged you."

Unbelievably Eamon smiled amid a little chuckle. God he must have dug deep for that.

"I am off now lad, if I am around Bury again and I run into you, I will stand you a brew."

"Where do you live Eamon?"

"Rochdale, but I enjoy a trip to Bury Market.

Obviously I don't get out much; the wife cannot be left on her own. I better get off, her sisters are at mine. Been there since this morning".

Eamon offered me his hand.

"Never mind your hand, come here".

I gave this poor man a heartfelt hug, and reminded him he will find me here every Wednesday and Friday at 1 pm.

"Okay Eamon, take care".

"You too Eamon".

I could not think of a damn thing to say to comfort him.

As Eamon slowly made his way through Millgate, again I was reminded how cruel and unfair life can be. I realise if every good person lived to 100 years old and died peacefully in their sleep, nature would have no place in that world. Plus we would have millions of folk living the life of saints. But this fact would be little comfort for poor Eamon. There will be no harm in me offering a little prayer for the poor chap.

46.

FACEBOOK

I cannot believe I am writing about Facebook. The reason being it forms part of the modern world most of us have been lured into. Being a fan of the old school ways, I never felt tempted to go beyond having a basic mobile phone that allows calls and texts only, not even a camera app. It was only when I needed to purchase a computer that would allow me to gain messages from my publisher that the situation arose, and, if I am honest, it proved not a bad thing. I hope never to become anything more than a casual browser but must admit it has reintroduced me to some long lost friends.

As an example, recently I received a friend request from a lady whose name seemed vaguely familiar. I was to spend a couple of weeks sending and receiving messages from Mrs Valerie Halliwell. Until one evening she messaged me enquiring about the Kavanagh family and relating her fond memories of them. Nothing for it.

"Hi Val, should I know you?"

Val very kindly reminded me she used 'go out' with our John when they were kids. Oh, my God. Brilliant. My memories of Val were of a lovely young lass who was a regular visitor to our Oxford Street home. First thing that struck me about Val was how quiet she was and when she did speak Val was very softly spoken. Val would later inform me she loved that 'big old house'. "So posh". Well that tickled me. Our old house was described in many ways: homely, cosy, spacious, but never once posh. It had been a long time since I had set eyes on Val. Last time we met she had married Steve Halliwell, then a struggling actor with a non-speaking part playing a courthouse copper in *Crown Court*, later to gain national treasure status in *Emmerdale* playing the part of 'Zak Dingle'. Steve enjoyed a pint and for a time was a regular of the Crown on Rochdale Road. My mate Derek Butterworth was a good friend to Steve in the early days and for a short time occupied the same house.

During the course of messaging one another I informed Val of where and when she could find me on market days on the occasions she was visiting her daughter who now resides in Bury. A week later I am sat with a couple of friends at Costa in the market square and who comes walking past, 'Dick Dastardly'. Sorry, don't know what came over me. Of course it was Val. And my God, she looks mighty fine. Slightly older than me but you could honestly assume she was two decades younger. The poor girl was shattered on account of the car journey from Leeds taking twice as long as it normally would, as the traffic was terrible.

"Look, sit down Val. This is Keith and this is Wendy. I will go get you a brew".

I could hardly wait to get back to have a chat with Val. When I returned with the drinks Val was chatting away with Keith and Wendy. Obviously the shy retiring girl had blossomed into a warm and confident lady. As Keith and Wendy took their leave, Val and me had a short while, before we would be joined by her daughter and granddaughter, both a credit to their proud Mum and Nan. In that short time Val and me engaged in a rich and enjoyable conversation that enlightened us both as to the quality of one another's life. Val for her part had worked really hard in the subjects she had a passion for. This resulted in her gaining a BA Hons Degree in Fine Art and a teaching position. The girl's an artist, wow!

After seeing some of her paintings I could see she was a damn good one at that.

"How do you like living in Leeds then?"

"It's good, but I miss Bury".

Leeds was obviously handy for Steve's work on *Emmerdale,* but with Steve being a Bury lad and Val a local lass, who knows.

Val informed me our John used to send her little love notes. Well, I cannot tell you how much that shocked me. I never knew our kid, apart from necessary form filling, had ever put pen to paper and definitely not for romantic declarations. You think you know all there is to know about some folk, but there you go. Will have some fun when I am down at John's again. Ha, ha.

Val was telling me how much she is looking forward to the upcoming reunion for our school St Gabriel's to celebrate its 60th anniversary.

"Won't it be grand," I said. "I cannot wait to finally meet up with Mr Tonge. It's only been 30 years".

"I know," Val said, "but I think we have to accept it won't be easy to recognise some folks, even old muckers".

"Don't they ask you to attach a name tag to your coat or jacket".

"Not sure Val, not sure if I fancy that. I don't mean to sound depressing, but truth is we have already lost a good few of our old school mates. All good folk, taken too soon".

Val admitted the news of Carol Wilcox passing really upset her.

"I know," I said, "what a lovely girl in every sense of the word. Reckon 90 per cent of the lads at Gabs were smitten with her. So sad. Well anyway we will have a grand old time in the evening at the Elizabethan Suite at the Town Hall. They reckon 400 folk will be attending. Cannot wait. Forgot to mention Val that I will be celebrating my 60th birthday this coming October so hope you and Steve can come along".

I have celebrated all my important landmark birthdays beginning with my 18th. I understand many folk would choose to seek more peaceful ways to celebrate, but personally I enjoy big get-togethers. (Any excuse). I know folk say it so often, it seems almost a tired statement, but bloody hell where have the years gone? It seems like yesterday my Mum was lovingly changing my nappy. Well, you know what I mean ha ha. Have to admit; for the most part life is sweet. I pray I have many good years left to enjoy this crazy upside down world. Death holds no fear for me, but I would so miss the warm touch and embraces from the many loving folk I am so lucky to call friends. Last words I promise. I know I have gone on in the past about us all getting more proactive with the old folk. Just a reminder that you could change someone's day from an expected lonesome struggle to get through, to a mood-changing realisation some folk do care. You will be well rewarded.

47.

THE BUS RIDE

It is Friday morning; I am aboard the 471 bus heading for Bury centre. I make this journey on average five times a week. If there is no one I know on board, I tend to look out the window to view the passing familiar panorama. Passing the remains of Ainsworth Finishing Company building, looking so forlorn, always saddens me. Not too long ago it was a hive of activity. Another reminder of our forsaken manufacturing industry.

It is spring and daffodils in full bloom decorate the roadside from the junction at Radcliffe Moor Road to the lights outside the Ainsworth Arms. Love the houses I pass on this part of the journey. Pre-war semi-detached and some detached. Large gardens front and rear, plenty for a fella such as myself to tend to his heart's content. Alas, my logical self knows my dream of owning one is exactly that 'a dream'. But you never know what is around the corner.

Coming up now is the relatively new Bolton Road Methodist Church and homes that occupy land that not too long ago was the home of my old club Elton Fold FC. Always brings a wry smile to my face as I remember when we first learned the land was earmarked for development. Well got on my high moral horse, penned a curt letter to the 'Readers Page' of the *Bury Times* going on with myself about the sports field being covered by a covenant, the previous owners dying wish for God's sake and no doubt the huge amount of money involved will easily win the battle. Well me and the other complainants were proved right. Cannot speak for the others but I for one ended up with egg on my face. The reason for this was the fabulous new sports ground provided by the developers, which included the best football pitch our fair town of Bury has ever seen for their amateur teams. Plus a lovely cricket pitch to warm the heart, a rounder's pitch and two brilliant tennis courts. I was not too proud to eat my humble pie. In fact I was more than happy.

On my left now we are approaching the famous 'Barracks', a building that once housed the even more famous Lancashire Fusiliers. Cannot help but feel a sense of loss. This building was part of my old postie round. On a couple of occasions I took time out to explore the museum that contained items from long ago conflicts. Being accompanied by a learned and instructive Colonel Glover was a pleasure indeed. Many local folk were upset when the war memorial monument was moved from its spiritual home outside the Barracks to Sparrow Park on Silver Street. Can really understand some folks anger, especially those who had scattered their loved ones ashes around the monument.

Having said all that, most of the folk I have discussed this with reckon overall it was a good move. Sparrow Park is very central, making easy access for all interested parties and the Hero's Cafe over the top of the new museum is the icing on the cake.

I realise many folk would take issue with this view. I accept that. I once saw a photo, I think it was on the 'Old Bury' website on Facebook, which showed the Barracks surrounded by hundreds of soldiers. The sight of a British 'Tommy' attired in his treasured khaki uniform will always to be sight that fills me with so many positive powerful emotions, words become useless. God knows we owe them so much.

Alighting on Market Street I enter Millgate to purchase the few items our John told me he needed. One of the items was a large bottle of Bells Whisky. On occasions John partakes of this revered tipple. Only once over the years was there any mishap as a result of this trait. For whatever reason, John had consumed more than his usual couple of glasses. After making his way unsteadily to his bathroom to take a pee, John lost his balance and fell into the adjacent bath.

After a couple of failed attempts at vacating the slippery prison he found himself, my brother drifted off into sweet oblivion whilst chuckling to himself. The following morning, as there was no answer, I let myself into John's flat. After a short worrying search, I found him sleeping the sleep of the contented, incredibly still with a gormless smile on his face. Well, I could not prevent myself breaking into a chuckle as I said loudly, "Wakey wakey our kid". Slowly he came back to himself. The two of us ended up cracking up as I helped him out of the bath.

"One too many last night Eam".

"No harm done cocker, I will make a cuppa".

After our John's I made my way to Costa in the square to meet one Martin Jones. I was looking forward to this. Martin and me went back to our childhoods. Me on Avondale Avenue, him on the Fairfield estate. Martin would be fetching along with him a couple of books on the 'American Civil War', this being his big passion. Being a country music fan, and many of this genre's artists recording songs reflecting this conflict, I was confident enough I could hold my side of our discussion concerning this subject. On Martin's arrival, after placing a mug of hot coffee in front of him, we began a really enjoyable chat. Martin's knowledge of the civil war is boundless. Love to hear passionate folk in full flow. I informed Martin about the year depicted on the date stone above my front door. 1861, the year the American Civil War broke out. And just may have been the trigger for my own passion for local history and to a lesser extent global history.

Listening to Martin recounting certain battles, his enthusiasm had me convinced I was taking part at times. After an hour and a half or so, Martin informed me he had to be somewhere.

"Before you go Martin, do you mind me asking you about your Riches to Rags story?"

Martin had no compunction in telling me this sorry tale. After an accident at work Martin received in the way of compensation an amount that could only be described as a life-changing sum. Martin, like me, came from poor working class stock. It was hard for me to get my head round how it was possible for such a fella to let all that slip through his fingers. Why was I not surprised by his answer?

"Drink and gambling".

To his credit Martin makes no excuses, he accepts he was a fool. What astonishes me in Martin's case is that he remains positive and optimistic about the future. Don't know about you, but most folk through the sheer sense of loss would become mentally crippled (including me). So admire the man.

After parting company with Martin I set off on the short journey to Big Jim's. Brilliant, our Pat's at the counter ordering his cup of tea, which has to be just so.

"Hi Pat".

"Go sit down, I will get these".

I know he is my brother but always feel a tingle of excitement in his company. He will always remain an inspiration to me. Love our chats and the way he accepts the physical blows he has received over the last few years. His latest battle being Parkinson's disease.

Sometimes my hero looks a little forlorn but his spirit remains tough as old rubber. Today I sense Pat is in good form. I decide I will tease him about an incident that came about a few days before. I had been after a certain CD of a group I first encountered in 1975 at the 5th International Festival of Country Music at the Empire Pool, Wembley, London accompanied by Pat and my mucker Bry Heys. We had already been entertained by stars such as Dolly Parton, Marty Robbins and Kitty Wells when a group of handsome young men took to the stage. These boys caused nothing short of a sensation with their original songs and the most infectious harmonies I had ever heard. Fabulous! Well! My search for the lads *Greatest Hits* was proving fruitless. Then a friend informed me they had seen it on Amazon for £68. Well, I just could not justify to Dawn spending that sort of money on a CD. Not when there were more pressing ventures. Sadly I put it out of my mind.

The week after my brew mate Leo turned up at Costa. After retrieving the coffee I had ordered we settled into our usual chats about anything that took our interest. After a while Leo just said, "Oh I almost forgot", then nonchalantly placed the *Greatest Hits of Tompall and the Glaser Brothers* on the table in front of me. I was dropped on when Leo said he had bought it on EBay for £10.

"You're joking. You little belter."

I could have kissed him. (Think I did). Made me feel mighty grand I can tell you. Thanks to Leo I am now boring everyone around my home by playing the *Tompall* CD nonstop for which I make no apologies. Two days before this meeting with our Pat I was down at his Nuttall Street home in order for him to copy my acquisition on to his wonderful 'Brennan'. This machine allows you to speed copy up to 5,000 CDs. Anyway, while the CD was being copied our Pat began inspecting the CD case.

"Don't believe it".

"Don't believe what?" I said.

"Reckon it's a copy".

"So what?" I said.

"Can't use it".

"What you on about?" I said.

"Cannot use it, it's illegal".

"God's sake Pat. I don't think the pearly gates will be slammed in your face for this little misdemeanour."

"No Eam, cannot do it".

I know Pat is a practicing Christian, but sometimes I end up throwing my hands in the air in frustration.

Well the day before this meeting I had phoned Pat to make sure he was okay for this get together.

"Hi Pat, you okay for tomorrow".

"Yeah, should be okay".

It was then I caught the music from my favourite *Tompall* track.

"Good tune you are playing there our kid".

"Oh yeah, didn't know what was playing, no problem our kid. See you tomorrow".

I then commenced to have a little chuckle to myself, thinking, "there is always hope".

48.

ST GABRIELS CELEBRATIONS

On 21 June I, along with many other former pupils, will be attending a celebratory get together in thanks for sixty years of endeavour by the teachers and management of a great school. Each member of my family, bar our Michael, passed through their hallowed doors. Our Mary was in the first batch of kids to begin their secondary education in 1954. After morning mass, folk will be invited to explore their old classrooms, gymnasium and assembly hall. Personally I am looking forward to inspecting the footy pitches, which hold so many great memories that remain so fresh in my mind, even now. Why do I already know, as my mind drifts back to those long gone days and I again walk on that same turf, my overriding emotion will be sadness. Not sure why it will be so, I just know it will. I really hope there will be a few folk from my year.

Many years ago I attended a reunion for our school at Radcliffe Civic Hall. I cannot remember seeing anyone from my year. My disappointment was eased by the attendance of my favourite teacher Mr Mick Tonge. I reckon my reluctance to address him any other way than 'Sir' caused him not a little amusement. Anything else seemed disrespectful, whether in my forties or not.

In the evening there is to be a meal and dance, which I am sure will be well attended as the 400 tickets on sale have more less all been sold. The fabulous Elizabethan Suite within the Town Hall is the venue. I so enjoy these special events. Nostalgia is such a powerful emotion. And to be sure all present will enjoy soaking up its welcome warming effect.

49.

LIFE ON A PENSION

"To be honest Eamon, I'm bored out of my head".

These words have been spoken to me by friends, who for one reason or another are no longer in gainful employment. To be honest, as much as I had empathy for them, these statements left me confused. Once I got over the feeling of being a 'kid wagging school', I absolutely loved being a free man, no longer being startled awake each morning by the heartless alarm clock and the fact I could spend the day exactly as I liked. Heaven! The secret lies in keeping your mind and body active. I cannot emphasise how important reading many good books meant to me. I don't exaggerate when I tell you I owe my sanity to the words from certain people's minds. I will always be in awe of anyone who lives their whole lives without any mental problems, I think must be pretty rare.

50.

APPROACHING THE BIG 60

Cannot believe I am only months off this milestone celebration. Just been looking through a couple of old albums, in some of the pictures I am a kiddie. Not sure if I should partake of this particular pastime. Don't know about you, but it always leaves me very emotional. Not even sure why. There is a saying 'youth is wasted on the young'. A little harsh but maybe true. I am really not sure if I would want to reinhabit my young self. All that angst, emotional storms, indecision and being governed by my loins.

Just writing that I have convinced myself I would refuse. It is something I hear from so many of my mature friends. They are now very relaxed in their own skins and on the whole very content. So it seems Mother Nature compensates your advancing years with wisdom and tranquillity. Not a bad exchange. I have celebrated every big birthday and I always end up emotional. I understand it is not everybody's cup of tea, but personally speaking, I love to have a room filled with friends and family all in high spirits and intent on lapping up the warm atmosphere that is always created when good solid folk are gathered.

Obviously this coming birthday will be that bit more special but also tinged with a little sadness. The reason for the sadness will be the absence of my best mucker "Mr Leach". This was to be a joint celebration for Paul and me. God I miss him so much. His photo will grace the stage and a couple of his favourite Big Country tracks will be played.

I will not allow things to become maudlin. Heaven knows Paul would not want that. Just hope I can hold it together whilst saying a few words in his honour. Obviously Paul's absence will without doubt add to my already emotional state. Hopefully by the time my birthday comes round, I will be able to think of Paul and smile. So wish for that, but I am not there yet.

These events tend to lend themselves to reflection. Most folk look back and accept certain events could have been handled better, but if you are sensible enough to learn from them, you are simply better equipped for future tests. Keeping yourself occupied in any way is beneficial to us all, placing yourself regularly into social situations. 'Touching base' with friends or sharing views with any folk you meet can be so rewarding. Happily, writing this book has kept me entertained for quite a while. One of my dreams in life is to manage eventually to knock a tune out, any simple old tune on my fender guitar. The fender being one in a long line of guitars I have possessed and spent many hours strumming away, never quite able to achieve anything that would please anyone's ears.

Just imagine you are sat on a beach, in a living room or even someone's garden, surrounded by a gang of friends, picking a guitar up and treating them to a song familiar to all assembled and played well enough to leave them unable to resist singing along. How good would that be? These are the sorts of events that remain in the memories of all concerned. One day!

The top wish in my 'Bucket List' for the last couple of years has been my trip of a lifetime. Ireland's west coast. Being a regular visitor to Dad's birthplace in Avoca and neighbouring towns of Arklow and Kildare, where my wife Dawn spent over twenty years, both her kids Tanya and Shane were born in Kildare. Tragically their Dad and Dawn's husband Sean was killed when hit by a car driven by two foreign visitors. Neither owned a licence. I enjoyed reading the book *McCarthy's Bar*. The story revolves around the author Pete McCarthy's decision to take a trip down Ireland's legendary west coast in an old Jalopy, Pete travels from town to town, relating his experiences so entertainingly you feel like you are on the trip with him.

The big attraction of a holiday along Ireland's west coast is the fact it retains the endearing quirkiness of old Ireland. As an example you could walk into a butcher's, or for that matter a cobblers, and be invited for a drink in the bar that will be located within the shop's building. Add to this the fact many places you will visit have not changed since the old days. The trip was all planned this year. Alas, setbacks concerning three members of the family's health were enough to shelve the project. No bother, there is always next year. I just would like to make the trip before the west coast succumbs to the blandness that accompanies the modern world.

51.

REFLECTION

More and more often of late, I seem to spend time in reflection. I find comfort from these necessary tranquil episodes. No background noise, only nature's music, periodic gifts to my relaxed mind. 'So good' to be free of the continued interference our modern life insists on. These times of peaceful reflection are becoming more of a necessity than a rejuvenating pastime. Modern life leaves little time for these important events. I realise for most folk there is little option when trying to earn a crust and raise children. Now though I am no longer in gainful employment, I enjoy a hectic social life, passing the time of day in good conversation with my fellow man and woman, is in my mind the best way to spend your time. So many interesting folk out there.

Lately much of my reflection centres on people I am so fond of and in some cases love. Good friends that are facing severe health problems. Frank O'Kane is a man I have revered for many years. His name would be whispered among my team-mates when they saw his name on our opposition's team sheet. His name struck fear into the hearts of our defenders. An uncompromising centre-forward, along with a steady determination to give his all in every game he played in. And believe me, his all was on most occasions more than enough. The thing with Frank is, off the pitch, he is the quintessential gentleman, able to switch from 'man possessed' to calm, thoughtful fella as smooth as you like. I got to know Frank when delivering to his home for a decade. 'Top man'. My opinion concerning another mate facing major health issues Paul Lomax were well documented in my first book. Love the man.

The sad truth is 'serious illness' is indiscriminate. No mercy is shown to the folk who have lived their lives in a way that has benefited all who are lucky enough to know them. I reckon my wife's past cancer condition, which has had a severe effect on her quality of life and with morphine being a necessary part of her pain control, has been my awakening to how tough each day can become.

"God bless them all".

52.

SO PROUD

With my brother Michael for company, the long arduous journey down to Guilford in Surrey to attend my son Ethan's passing out parade for the army was made almost enjoyable. The fact a few of our favourite records were played on the radio, accompanied by our less than decent backing vocals, helped our cause. We would be meeting up in Guildford with Ethan's Mum Debra, my ex-wife, our daughter Megan, her half-sister Danika, Deb's brother and his wife Steph, and Ethan's girlfriend Louise. Now and then I feel the need to check my ramblings. I know our Michael loves me but he also loves tranquil moments to contemplate. Over the years I have learned to judge his moods. Once we entered Surrey I was really taken with the passing views, gorgeous countryside, and intermittent glimpses of fabulous houses in their own grounds, partly obscured by dense clusters of mature trees. To me these houses had an 'aura' about them that invited me to 'come and explore'. If only!

Arriving at our destination at around 8pm, we wearily made our way with our overnight bags to check in. Twenty minutes later we were down at the restaurant. Apart from one stop to grab a coffee and a bag of nuts, we had had nothing. With hunger driving us we needed to seek advice on how we should proceed.

The chef appeared and promptly informed me and our kid the restaurant had just closed and professional pride forbade him from offering the meagre leftovers. Me and our kid would have answered that those leftovers to the two of us resembled sumptuous morsels that had our mouths watering in anticipation. Our Michael was priceless in these situations. After informing the chef he understood his reluctance, but as he was a regular patron of Holiday Inns, he would appreciate it if the chef would comply. Well to cut a long story short, we dined like kings. Remember now why I love our kid.

The following morning we met up with the others, hugs and greetings all round. We set off for the army base. After we were checked through by a couple of soldiers I would not pick an argument with, we set off to seek refreshments. By the time we exited the Spar shop the heat from the sun had become almost unbearable. Our collective thoughts went to the parading soldiers that would be clad in thick khaki uniforms. 'God bless 'em'. We made our way slowly across the parade to take our seats in what looked like football stands at the far end of the parade ground. The atmosphere was electric with families and friends getting more and more excited at the prospect of seeing their sons and mates parading with as much pride as was now swelling in all our assembled chests.

After what seemed like a lifetime, our chatter was silenced by the army band striking up. We then caught sight of our boys in the distance entering the arena from the far corner. Oh my, these proud young men settled into orderly columns directly in front of us. I looked across at Deb, tears rolling down her face (not just me then).

A couple of hours passed where the lads completed various manoeuvres using their rifles. The parade ended with our boys marching past us with their faces turned towards us. As we focussed on our son, Deb and me were once again consumed by too much emotion to contain. Well, no matter, these times allowed no shame.

With my Son Ethan.

My son Ethan is thriving within the family-like fold that is the British Army. My daughter Megan is enjoying training to be a psychiatric nurse. My eldest son Lee seems content in his work as a plasterer. What I would like to know is, does the worry for their welfare ever subside?

Ethan's proud family!

53.

APATHY THE MODERN CURSE

Apathy. Even the word emits weariness, I really do not wish to come across as some deluded Evangelist, I am in no position to do so. Alas, my concerns for the way of life I was raised in, and will always hold dear, seem to me at times in danger of becoming a way of life only remembered by us older folk. In itself this is not something to be too worried about. The worry comes with what seems to be replacing it.

Apathy should be resisted for what it represents, a modern day pestilence. Examples of its effect have now become almost impossible to avoid. It seems to me at times folk are hell bent on turning our green and pleasant land into a litter-strewn sewer. I know that sounds a little too dramatic but it drives me mad. Take this morning, heading for my 9am doctor's appointment, travelling the short distance along Bury Road that takes in the petrol station opposite my home to Morrisons Supermarket, I passed enough litter to half fill a dust waggon. Boarding the 471 bus to Bury later and having to remove the remnants of a half-eaten burger and three empty drink cans did nothing to improve my mood.

The last part of my journey leading to our John's which takes me along East Street, Heywood Street and Killon Street hardly improved my mood. What is going on in these folk's minds, absolutely no consideration for anything or anyone that would incur any effort on their part? The 'can't be arsed' brigade. God I hate that statement.

It is so rare now to see our young folk engaged in verbal interaction. They are either on their phones or staring blankly at their precious screens. On the occasions I witness them having a good old chat, I feel an almost irresistible urge to approach them and say, "Isn't that better?" This is still a grand island but the things we hold dear have to be defended.

There is no shame in showing pride in our fabulous history, our quirky traditions and habits. It is a way of life once the envy of the world. Our ancestors were willing to make the ultimate sacrifice to protect a way of life they felt justified their love. I love my country. My dream is that our pathetic political parties grow a pair and at last realise the folk who have lived on these shores for generations have been sorely let down by their weak leadership. 'Rant over'.

Maybe just upset after watching probably the most moving film based on a true story I have ever had the privilege to view. *The Scarlet and the Black* starring Gregory Peck moved me so much it brought me to tears. These days that would not be too difficult. It seems I get emotional at the drop of a hat. Even so, I defy any of you to watch this film and not end up in the same state.

I won't reveal too much. It is enough to say it is the story of a man's love for his fellow man and his enemies. It will renew your faith in mankind. A truly rare quality in today's 'me' world. Kindness, empathy, tolerance and above all love hopefully will once more take their rightful place in our damaged society.

Please forgive me for my confusing meanderings. A big thank you for purchasing this book. I really hope you have enjoyed it for the most part. If you have, obviously we would have much in common. Even if you haven't, if we meet let me know. You will know where to find me. It would be appreciated.

WASTE

So short, so sweet, it seems was our time
Your pain on parting, entwined with mine.
Confusion for reasons, invade my mind
Ones that answer, not easy to find.
As our love so fragile it could not withstand
The spectre of past love, merely lending a hand.
Honesty evades us, mean thoughts all that's found
They cut and corrupt us, though make not a sound.
No denying the past, it happened, they're here
Both yours and mine, but shed not a tear.

They pose not a threat, left alone they'd retreat
In search of their own love, they are destined to seek.
Let them rest in our past, when we meet it's as friends
The way that it should be, no need to defend.
At times life is hard, our own problems abound
Let us seek no more, with reasons unsound.
To offer a hand, seems the right thing to do
With the lend of an ear 'folks' hope' you renew.
Your eyes betray fear resides deep inside
There is a need to air, what you seek to hide.

The turmoil within you, I so understand
To draw the line, without being unkind.
My judgement with lines seem so off the mark
Here alone in our room, I sit in the dark.
In the gloom I see clearly, so many mistakes
Among good intentions, there is selfish to take.

Realisation a good thing, no matter how hard
The facts lie unspoken, we choose to discard.
My poor attempt of living life true
Leaves only despair, in loved ones like you.
As much as it grieves me, cannot change the past
The future, my salvation, my colours to the mast.

ND - #0207 - 270225 - C0 - 234/156/9 - PB - 9781780914589 - Gloss Lamination